To Rita Jacobs,

"Let this book bring clarity to any questions you may have had concerning death and dying. It's designed to bring comfort and hope to all who read it. May it help you to encourage others as well."

Eddie Jackson

1 THES. 5:6-11

THE LIFE OF THE DEAD

Everyone Included

Dr. Eddie B. Jackson

authorHOUSE®

AuthorHouse™
1663 Liberty Drive
Bloomington, IN 47403
www.authorhouse.com
Phone: 1-800-839-8640

First published by AuthorHouse 4/29/2011

ISBN: 978-1-4567-1682-0 (sc)
ISBN: 978-1-4567-1684-4 (hc)
ISBN: 978-1-4567-1683-7 (e)

Library of Congress Control Number: 2011901914

Printed in the United States of America

This book is printed on acid-free paper.

Certain stock imagery © Thinkstock.

Dedicated To ...

... my wife Jean, who stayed at the altar of prayer
ten long years, praying for my deliverance from
the secular lifestyle I was practicing.
But you did not stop there. Your Christian walk has
been a tremendous encouragement to me.
I love you!

... my only daughter, Teresa, who is a shining example of motherhood.

... my three granddaughters, Jenna, Moriah, and Anna.
I am proud to be your grandfather.
I love each of you!

ACKNOWLEDGEMENTS
(IN RANDOM ORDER)

I wish to give thanks to the Reverend Robert (Bob) Schultz and his wonderful wife, Anne. You both have been a tremendous blessing to Jean and me during the many years we have known each other and during the times we have ministered alongside each other. Special thanks for taking time to read and critique the first draft of the manuscript for this book. Your constructive criticism set me on the path I was seeking.

Also, I wish to express special thanks to our dear neighbor, Mrs. Martha Henry, one of the world's greatest and most dedicated schoolteachers of all time. Your critique of the second draft of this book encouraged me to the extent that I felt ready to pass it on to my final critic, my wife Jean.

To those of you who encouraged me to put my observations concerning the life of the dead into book form, thanks. Your encouragement motivated me to the degree necessary to provoke me to share with others on this broad scale the insight the Holy Spirit has given me.

Virginia House, my dear sister-in-law, thank you for exercising your gift of proofreading. I needed your skilful and keen eyes.

To Dr. B. Jean Jackson, my lovely wife and one of the greatest literary critics I have been blessed to know, many, many thanks! I thank you for tolerating the disruption I brought to your sleep as I would come to bed so many nights at late, late hours. Thank you for taking time to read, critique, and edit my final draft. Once you finished with it, I felt confident it was ready to convey my thoughts to its readers. Last, yet first and foremost, I praise our God of all life and creation for the gift of this work.

Love you all,
Ed Jackson

CONTENTS

PREFACE

This book is borne out of many years of attempting, on my part, to console people during their times of bereavement. Such ministerial duty prompted me to pursue thoughts and questions that had accumulated in my head. Those thoughts and questions began when I was very young.

After becoming a minister of the gospel of Jesus Christ, I began to search the Bible in an attempt to learn what God says about the life of the dead. The more I studied and searched the Scriptures, the greater was the enlightenment I received in that sphere of eschatology. My study and research led to my taking a different path in offering consolation to the bereaved.

It was not easy to settle on the idea of sharing my convictions with the general public. I had heard great biblical students, renowned preachers and teachers, as well as lay persons say things about the activities, the state or status, and the after-life in general pertaining to the deceased. I knew those people could not all be wrong. Without any intention of proving or disproving what I had been taught, or the matters that had been brought to my attention, I began to study and listen closely to what the Bible had to say.

My attempt to share what the Holy Spirit has revealed to me concerning the life of the dead necessitated the approach I have taken. I strongly believe that, in the end, no one will consider this book to be contrary to the everyday expressions we hear uttered as it pertains to the status or activities of the deceased. I have merely attempted to put biblical truth in a perspective that can be readily grasped. But for the most part, many Christians are saying basically the same things in different words. However, some of those words are not quite the way the Bible puts them. I believe my approach paints a more vivid picture relating to God's purpose regarding man's natural death and his arrangement of the life of the dead.

I have made it a point to use only the *Holy Bible* as a source of reference to paint this picture on the canvas of my observation. I do not believe God intends for man to interpret the Bible. I am of the persuasion that the Bible interprets itself. Our task is to listen closely to what God has already said. No new revelation is written herein. But I believe accents of color will come more into focus as you read this book, giving you a richer appreciation of the truth of this sphere of eschatology.

At the risk of sounding a bit redundant, I purposely repeat certain points in hope of keeping the reader's mind focused on critical points.

May the richest of God's blessings come upon you.

Eddie B. Jackson, D.D.
Bishop and Vice President
Lighthouse Full Gospel Church, Pentecostal,
Incorporated, International

Senior Pastor, Seaside Lighthouse Full Gospel Church
Monterey Peninsula, California

August 14, 2010

Introduction

Other books in circulation address life after death as well as other aspects of eschatology. But that is not the primary aim of this book. My desire and intention are to call the reader's attention to passages of biblical scripture that reveal and enlighten a person concerning the true and indisputable status of the dead. This aim has come about as a result of counseling the bereaved as well as listening to others whose convictions are not in accordance with biblical teaching.

Many arguments pertaining to the life of the deceased are merely philosophical in content. Much is based on traditional reasoning that has been handed down through generations and has gone unchallenged for biblical accuracy. The perception that many people have concerning death has caused them to be very dreadful and even fearful of dying. This book points to those passages of Scripture that will set people free from such fear and dreadfulness.

For many, death is a really bad or taboo word. And people such as life insurance agents, cemetery plot sales representatives, and the like refrain from using the words *death*, *dead*, *deceased*, and so on when speaking with a client or potential client. This book should help the reader to accept and acknowledge death openly. I believe that almost anyone who reads this book will cease fearing death.

I have no intention of presenting any new revelations. I merely point out things that are fairly plain in Scripture but apparently have been overlooked or misinterpreted. What makes the difference is that I bring pertinent passages of scripture together in a manner that perhaps better connects the puzzle or mystery of the life of the dead. At most, one needs only take several passages out of context to cause a misunderstanding of a biblical truth. I have observed that denominational doctrines are often established upon misinterpretation of passages of Scripture. Those negatives have been considered and are addressed from a biblical standpoint that is likely to put every believer at ease. This work shall leave no doubt in one's mind that after the fall of man, death is the best thing to be given to us, save the shed blood of Jesus Christ.

The whole of the argument of this book is Bible centered, and I understand and acknowledge that no revelation of truth of God's word is given apart from the work of the Holy Spirit. Therefore, all understanding of the Bible depends on illumination by the Holy Spirit. This means that not only has it been necessary for me to pray and write under the anointing of the Holy One, but I have also had to allow the Bible to interpret itself.

All who have departed this life have experienced death except Enoch, who walked with God, and Elijah, who was translated from earth via the chariot of the Lord. Even if it is only when all are changed from mortal to immortal, we are going to experience death. Thus, the best time to talk about death is now. It has been said that the two inescapable things in this country are taxes and death. Some have left this world without paying taxes, but death is another matter. Let's face it: all are destined to die. But this book helps the reader to not only understand that truth but also to receive death as a means of taking off mortality and corruption. It is my hope and belief that the bereaved and the potentially bereaved will be consoled and comforted after reading this book. Hopefully, the truth of the Scriptures indicated in this work will cause any fear of death to dissipate as one allows the Bible to interpret itself.

It has been my intention to take into account the whole counsel of God as it relates to death and the life of the dead. As the reader is reminded of biblical quotations pertaining to the subject matter, he or she should be able to better understand the fact that there is absolutely no time span between death and the resurrection of a Christian. Please keep in mind that the points contained herein are not derived through philosophical reasoning. And with this in mind, know that only the Bible can give us proper insight into the life of the dead.

Upon consideration of the truth given from the pages of the Bible, one shall be able to more clearly see that no insensitivity is involved on God's part regarding suffering and dying. The fact that God's ways are not our ways is simplified in *The Life of the Dead*.

Although the subject is mentioned, I do not attempt to prove or disprove the argument on creation versus evolution. I do, however, iterate and reiterate (in Chapter Seven) certain viewpoints in support of creation and procreation as a matter of food for thought, so to speak. It is included primarily for the skeptic, yet in my opinion it is interesting to practically any reader. I have made the assumption that anyone who does not believe in creation also does not believe in the resurrection of the dead from a biblical perspective. Evangelism, may I also add, is not the main thrust of this work, though I pray the biblical truth of it will serve as a catalyst to lead many to the decision of accepting eternal life through Jesus Christ.

The reader can expect to get a better understanding of what death is all about above and beyond the mere thought of the deceased simply becoming absent from the body and being present with the Lord. A vivid picture is painted that reveals the fact that death involves being totally unable to function in any capacity of the human design.

In addition, I also elaborate on the reason saints are called upon to sacrifice and suffer for Christ's sake as part of my attempt to establish and prove my points. Though brief and concise, the points being brought to the reader's attention make it easier to understand and accept one's call as a believer to bear his or her cross. It is observed that God has a precise purpose for everything he does.

During the course of reading this book, a person is likely to gain a more vivid picture of life after death. The picture one is expected to gain will allow him or her to overcome the dread, fear, or resentment of death and acquire the right perspective on death after life in this world and life after death in the world to come.

Perhaps the foregoing statement sounds a bit confusing considering the way it is presented. But as you read the book, everything shall become crystal clear. The otherwise strange talk becomes recognized as proper. It should cause one to see life and death from God's perspective rather than from the traditional viewpoint of most people.

As the focus of man's earthly purpose following the fall, which this book addresses, becomes clearer, it is expected that one will better understand the love, mercy, grace, and wisdom of God. The truth contained herein will make one better able to see what God is doing and thus cause a person to be more willing and excited about joining God in his work of reconciliation and more accepting of the timing of death for any of our loved ones, friends, and even one's self. This book gives, or at least enhances, the conviction that death is not our enemy, as many seem to think.

The Life of the Dead is written in simple language and is very easy to understand. As a convenience, most biblical references are quoted in full the first time they are mentioned; occasionally, a quote is repeated when references are made to other places of the book.

All quotes are made from the King James Version.

Chapter Six is included as a survey or capsule of the book. The purpose for Chapter Six is to convey the essence of the whole book in the form of a recapitulation. The idea is to provide enough information to cause one to readily become consoled and comforted in the hour of bereavement. That is to say, the chapter is included for the benefit of those who need consolation but who do not necessarily have time at the moment to read the whole book. It does, however, include some points not mentioned elsewhere in this work.

Finally, an epilogue is included as Chapter Seven. It contains a brief discussion concerning evolution versus creation. This discussion is made on behalf of the skeptics and those of whom the skeptics have confused. It is understood that many skeptics claim dogmatically the idea that the world and the hosts therein came about by chance. Chapter Seven is neither established nor designed for the purpose of convincing those skeptics that evolution in the sense of Darwin's theory is proper or improper. It merely includes enough discussion to offer food for thought to those who have allowed the proevolutionists to confuse them.

CHAPTER ONE

Death and Its Cause

DEFINITION OF DEATH

I wish to establish up front the definition of death as it pertains to the primary discussion in this book. Therefore, I will provide illustrations and examples to ensure the reader gets a good understanding of the definition of death.

Word dictionaries such as *Merriam-Webster's* define death as "a permanent cessation or ceasing of all vital functions." Such a broad definition can apply to anything that once lived but is now dead. This means that anything or anyone that ceases to possess the ability to function as it was designed and constructed to operate during its life cycle is considered dead, period. But when we add the spiritual aspect to the equation, so to speak, the definition is extended quite a bit.

The meaning of the word *dead* in its noun form refers to that which has been totally deprived of the ability to function as it was designed or constructed. This means that the person, thing, or whatever the animated object may have been is no longer able to serve its primary purpose.

We, of course, also have the verb form of *death,* which is the term *die.* "To die" simply refers to the loss of the vitality necessary to function as a person or thing was designed. Everything that dies obviously has at some point been alive. This means that absolutely nothing is dead that has never been alive. We sometimes use the term "dead as a rock." The design and function of a rock has never included animation, growth, or the production of anything. Sure, a rock might give off certain gases or minerals, but that is because part of its composition includes minerals and gases. But the rock itself has never been alive.

I grew up in the state of Mississippi. Located there in the town of Flora is a petrified forest park. It is reported that the forest has been petrified for more than thirty-six million years. The park includes a museum with collections of petrified items from various places around the globe. All the items in the museum were once alive, and those items serve a purpose today. But their original purposes were not to become displays for a museum.

There is always a major separation involved in dying. Something has to become severed or separated or broken in order for death to occur. Think about the landline telephones some of us still have at home and most workplaces. It is not uncommon for someone to pick up the receiver and, if they hear no dial tone, to utter, "The phone is dead." The telephone may still be intact, but if it will not transmit and receive, it is thought of as being dead. Why? Because however temporary the situation may be, the phone has lost its ability to function as it was designed. That is the idea in a nutshell of something being dead.

Again, separation is involved in all instances of death, especially when it comes to the human being. Literally or figuratively, *death*, *dead*, and any other derivative of the root word speak of some key element or component having been removed or broken to the extent that the object does not work for the purpose it was designed and constructed. The petrified stuff in the park in Mississippi attracts many tourists, but it was not originally designed for such purpose. If the vegetation were still growing in a forest, we would declare it to be alive.

With reference to a vehicle, you might hear someone say, "The battery is dead" or "The engine is dead." They would probably mean that the battery has lost its ability to provide power to turn the engine or perhaps that fuel is not getting to the engine properly. Either way, purpose is not being fulfilled.

One of the most common expressions concerning an engine or motor when someone wants it to cease functioning for a moment is, "Kill the engine." That means do what is necessary to separate the motor from its source of energy or power. Such separation causes the combustion or other means of power to cease, and in turn the engine or motor will die or stop operating.

What is a common term for the end of a thoroughfare? "Dead end" is the main one we use. We use that term because the street ceases to go any farther. Streets are pathways or thoroughfares. And when one ceases to extend any farther, right at that point it becomes a dead end. That is to say, the street functioned as a pathway until it ended.

All life upon planet Earth comes to a dead end at some point. If we stop and think about it, we will probably agree there is nothing bad or unusual about life, as we know it, coming to an end. The one big exception is when one follows the path of the rich man that the Bible tells about at Luke 16:22b–24. It says, "… the rich man also died, and was buried; and in hell he lift up his eyes, being in torments, and seeth Abraham afar off, and Lazarus in his bosom. And he cried and said, Father Abraham, have mercy on me, and send Lazarus, that he may dip the tip of his finger in water, and cool my tongue; for I am tormented in this flame." This was not his fate because he was rich; he died without having the salvation of the Lord Jesus. And it is up to each of us to not allow our departure to result in our ending up where the rich man went. Hell was not where the rich man died. He went to hell because he had never become born again following his death through the fall of Adam. Thus, before he died physically, he was already dead spiritually. Being assigned to hell was his second death (Rev. 21:8).

Apostle Paul of the Bible gives us a solid clue at Romans 5. From verse 17 through verse 19, we find, "For if by one man's offence death reigned by one; much more they which received abundance of grace and of the gift of righteousness shall reign in life by one, Jesus Christ. Therefore as by the offence of one judgment came upon all men to condemnation; even so by the righteousness of one the free gift came upon all men unto justification of life. For as by one man's disobedience many were made sinners, so by the obedience of one shall many be made righteous." Here Paul refers to man's first death, which took place when Adam fell in sin in the Garden of Eden. Man died spiritually the very day he disobeyed God. Paul says "judgment" came upon all men to condemnation. And at Revelation 21:8, the Bible tells of eternal judgment coming upon all unrepentant men. It is the irreversible separation from God that is here being pronounced upon those who reject the salvation of Christ.

There are two categories of death I wish to discuss concerning the human being. They are in no way interchangeable, though we sometimes treat them as such. The categories I wish to discuss are natural death and spiritual death.

THE NATURAL DEATH OF MAN

Because sin entered the world and death comes by sin, God has purposed that we all must die physically as well as spiritually. Romans 5:12 tells us, "Wherefore, as by one man sin entered into the world, and death by sin; and so death passed upon all men, for that all have sinned." Most people are not fond of the thought of having to separate from their physical bodies, especially if it is in good health and they are at peace. But the Bible says death is passed upon all men. The above passage speaks of spiritual death. I have heard some teach something to this effect: "Because spiritual death has been passed upon all, God has destined all men to die naturally as well as spiritually." But however it is stated, all have died spiritually: it happened when Adam died. And all who have not already died shall one day die naturally or physically as well. But it is the second spiritual death that we should strive to never experience (Rev. 20:14; 21:8).

Seeing that death is passed upon everyone, let us not be so reserved when it comes to uttering the word *death*. Plenty of people do not believe in spiritual death, but as for the natural death, I have heard of only a few who do not believe it is inevitable for all. The few I have in mind belong to a religious group that I do not hear much about anymore. As a child, I heard my parents talking about them. I cannot recall their true name, but their nickname was the "Never Diers." Their faith led them to believe that people of their religion would not die. I recall my parents saying that every time one died, the others would beat on the person's corpse in an attempt to awaken him. They would say he or she just got lazy and would not wake up. I remember laughing, thinking they all would get lazy one day along the way.

Excluding people like the Never Die-ers all of us have become convinced that we will die sooner or later. But just because dying is the last thing on earth we do, there is no reason for it to be the last thing we talk about. And surely we should not wait until we lose someone close to us before we face the reality that everyone has to die. Right now is the best time to face and talk about the inevitable fate that awaits every one of us. We need to break the silence concerning the subject and the matters surrounding death.

Have you noticed that people such as insurance agents and cemetery plot sales representatives almost always avoid the use of the word *death* or any derivative thereof? They make statements such as, "*Should* something happen to you …" If you did not know better, you could end up thinking you have a decent chance of evading the fate of death. But I wish to say to all of us to not worry about death. I have come to the conclusion that death is only the completed action of dying. And dying is not a bad event, nor is it a bad experience. Think about it. The only registered regrets we ever get come from the living—not the dead. The Bible tells us of a rich man lifting up his eyes in hell after his death, but the point of the story does not pertain to his death (Luke 16:19–23). It is about life after death. Ending up in hell did not stem from his dying, but rather from his life before his natural death.

The natural death of man happens as a result of the spirit leaving his body, or the house in which he lives. Death in every case involves a type of separation. I heard Dr. Myles Munroe refer to the body as an earth suit. But the body or earth suit or house does not function as a component of the human being apart from its union with the spirit and soul. And when the spirit leaves the body, the corpse dies physically. This is because the body, the spirit, and the soul are designed to operate only when they are unified. (I cannot overemphasize this principle. If we ignore it, confusion sets in when we consider what we call the "hereafter life.") In fact, human life is the result of three existing factors. In other words, we are tripartite (three-parted) beings, consisting of body, spirit, and soul. This simple truth actually holds the key that unlocks much of the mystery concerning the life of the dead. Do not forget that we are created to function in a body. Yes, the Bible reveals that we are spirit beings living in a body. But if any one of the three major components of man is removed, the others cease to function as a living human being. I am in no way suggesting that there comes a point when a man's spirit, which is the very core of his being, ceases to exist, but the spirit of man ceases to function as a human being. I find no biblical basis that supports the "soul-sleeping" doctrine, so that is not what I have in mind. But I am stating that man's spirit is only in a mode of functioning when it is united with a body. It is at the point of unity of spirit and body that man becomes a living soul. Think about it. The very phrase "man became a living soul" as recorded in Genesis 2:7 infers that a change takes place. Hence, man was something other than a living soul before he became "a living soul." He was a lifeless body.

We should keep in mind that physical or natural death does not represent the end of life as it pertains to the spirit of man. It only means the end of our corruptible bodies. Natural death is the threshold to our crossover from the realm of time into the realm of eternity. Natural death for a saint of God merely causes him or her "to be absent from the body and to be present with the Lord" (2 Cor. 5:8).

The natural body, of course, is left behind when the spirit departs from it. Who needs it anyway? It is contaminated with sin and corruption. God caused it to be cut off from the Tree of Life; we learn that at Genesis 3:22. The passage reads, "And the Lord God said, Behold, the man is become as one of us, to know good and evil: and now, lest he put forth his hand, and take also of the tree of life, and eat, and live for ever." That is the summation of why the body dies. But it turns out to be a good thing. It was out of the love and mercy of God that man was cut off from the Tree of Life in the Garden of Eden. Who wants to live forever without the ability to function in the very activities for which he is designed? Eternal depression is not at all inviting. I will elaborate on that a bit more shortly.

We are talking about life and death. For us, death involves a form and status of life. Like the telephone analogy, when the man lacks the Father-to-son relationship with God, he is spiritually dead. He may still be housed in his physical body and doing well from a natural point of view, but nothing good takes place when one is separated from the spirit of God. The main purpose of our creation was to be connected to the spirit of God. Take that away, and one becomes spiritually dead! All becomes vanity.

We read at Luke 11:25, "Jesus said unto her, I am the resurrection, and the life: he that believeth in me, though he was dead, yet shall he live." (Later, we shall establish from biblical revelation that there is no downtime or span between death and the resurrection of the dead.) The above particular truth pertains only to those who die in Christ. He who dies the natural death without being in Christ is damned forever. The good news, however, is that such does not have to be your lot. Jesus came and died that you might live. Every living soul has a right to the "Tree of Life." Jesus is that spiritual tree.

THE CAUSE AND REASON BEHIND NATURAL DEATH

Obviously, there is a cause and a reason behind both spiritual and natural death. We have already observed that death was passed upon all men. It is also a fact that death entered the world by way of sin, and all have sinned. But we have not discussed the precise cause and the divine reason for death being passed upon all men. Let us do that next.

Observing Genesis 2:16–17, we see, "And the Lord God commanded the man, saying, Of every tree of the garden thou mayest freely eat: but of the tree of the knowledge of good and evil, thou shalt not eat of it: for in the day that thou eatest thereof thou shalt surely die." In other words, God meant that man would die at the moment he ate of the tree, and it did happen at the precise moment man disobeyed God. Adam's spirit man, as we would call it, was severed from union and fellowship with the spirit of God. And it did not happened to Adam only, but to everyone who would come from his loins. Plus, it happened to Eve. However, death did not come upon her because of the sin of Adam—she was outside the loins of Adam when he ate of the forbidden fruit. Eve died spiritually and became prone to die naturally because of her personal disobedience. She was aware of the fact that consumption of the fruit was forbidden by God (Gen. 3:3).

An important point I wish to make is that the sin of disobedience did not cause man to die physically. Of course, disobedience (sin) was the perpetrator, but it was not the cause and reason for the natural death of man. God did not address natural death with Adam. The act of sin brought about immediate death from a spiritual standpoint, which involves man's spirit becoming separated from the spirit of God. Sin, or disobedience, is what destroyed the relationship and severed the communion and the fellowship between man and God. But it was God's merciful judgment that brought about physical death. I hear biblical preachers and teachers speak as though natural death was promised in the commandment that Adam was given pertaining to the forbidden fruit. That does not at all appear to be the case.

The love and mercy of God comes into focus when we observe Genesis 3:22–24: "And the Lord God said, Behold, the man is become as one of us, to know good and evil: *and now, lest he put forth his hand, and take also of the tree of life, and eat, and live for ever:* Therefore the Lord God sent him forth from the garden of Eden, to till the ground from whence he was taken. So he drove out the man; and he placed at the east of the garden of Eden Cherubims, and a flaming sword which turned every way, to keep the way of the tree of life" (emphasis added). The above passage within itself reveals that it was the goodness of God that kept man from living forever in a state of sinfulness, which would automatically result in eternal separation from God. It is right there in this passage that God sanctioned natural death.

Let us keep in mind that God did not create man for the mere purpose of man's enjoying the pleasure of being alive. No matter how many times a claim to the contrary is made, the human being cannot experience lasting peace and joy outside of a connection to God. We are simply out of place, so to speak, when we are apart from him. He created man for the joy and glory of God himself. Isaiah 43:7 declares, "Even every one that is called by my name: for I have created him for my glory, I have formed him; yea, I have made him." But being the good and merciful and gracious God he is, he has seen fit that life should be pleasant and delightful to us. And because of his mindfulness of us, he made it possible for man to enjoy life through his natural senses.

Our Lord is unlike people who declare that they love their birds, their fish, and so on. They claim to truly love those creatures, but they keep the birds that are designed to fly and roam the heavenly sky caged up for life. They keep the fish that are designed to swim rivers and seas restricted in almost no water in comparison to the vast habitat they were created to occupy. The bottom-line reason behind people doing things like this has to do with their being more interested in self-gratification than in the lives and joy of their pets. Our God is not like that. He has seen fit to make provisions for our natural comfort as well as our spiritual joy. Yet, we exist for his delight!

The pleasant and delightful life God has ordained for man cannot be realized apart from the spirit of man being in relationship with the spirit of God and having communion and fellowship with him, as well. Man cannot have those things apart from a Father-to-son relationship with him. God so much wants to realize the potential glory and honor and wonderful communion and fellowship of mankind that he established the whole Bible, and gave his only begotten son, and he has made available to us the person of the Holy Spirit (also called the Comforter), all to draw, lead, and guide us back to the Father. Had he not done that, we would be in much trouble—a most miserable people from the first person to the last one.

My thoughts go to one of the many passages of Scripture that reflects the love and concern that God has for man. This passage is itself enough to establish that God's love and concern led to his having mercy on fallen man. At John 3:16 we are told, "For God so loved the world, that he gave his only begotten Son, that whosoever believeth in him should not perish, but have everlasting life." What I have come to see and understand and highly appreciate is that, out of his love and concern for us, God ordained that we die a natural death so that we could be resuited in a body designed to dwell in his presence throughout eternity. (Keep in mind that the fallen and contaminated body is no longer suitable. God has never attempted to save it.)

Take close notice of Genesis 3:22, quoted earlier: "And the Lord said,

Behold, the man is become as one of us, to know good and evil: and now, *lest he put forth his hand, and take also of the tree of life, and eat, and live for ever*" (emphasis added). Of course, we know God is not saying the fall of man has resulted in man's becoming *Elohim* (God). This verse does, however, pose some difficulty in biblical interpretation. But now is not the time for a theological dissertation concerning the matter, which would draw our attention away from the primary point I wish to make. What we want to notice closely in the above passage is the fact that God said "lest he put forth his hand, and take also of the tree of life, and eat, and live for ever." This shows that sin did not automatically carry a sentence of natural death, as so many have thought. Had sin meant automatic physical death, Adam would have died naturally at the same time he died spiritually. At Genesis 2:17b, we read, "... for in the day that thou eatest hereof thou shalt surely die." Man's disobedience brought spiritual separation and engendered man's ultimate physical death. Of course, God set the boundaries and consequences, but man made the choices.

God, as I alluded to earlier, out of his goodness toward man, had mercy on him and cut him off from the Tree of Life. As an intelligent creature, man—if allowed further access to the Tree of Life—would have been totally without a moral compass, and such state would have had no end. All of his imagination would have been evil, wickedness, and total vanity. Just think of the evil, the wickedness, and the immoralities we have seen escalate during the past thirty to forty years. And then try to imagine what an eternity of such behavior, escalating to no end, would mean.

Most people actually want to know why we all have to die. Some answer the question with short essays and others by simply saying, "I don't know." I wish to be included with those of the short essays. The answer is simple and brief: our bodies do not have access to the natural "tree of life." In a nutshell, that is why we have to die physically. We have no available means of remaining alive forever, though man seems to be trying to bring it to pass.

God evicted Adam and Eve from the Garden of Eden where the Tree of Life existed. (Whether or not that natural tree still exists, I have no idea). As we looked at Genesis 3:22–24, it became apparent that man has no means of sustaining his natural body because the Tree of Life is no longer available. Thus, being unable to partake of the tree, the natural body lives a short span and then perishes. The human body breaks down and returns to dust, and the human spirit returns to God from whence it came. We learn at Ecclesiastes 12:7 that "Then shall the dust return to the earth as it was: and the spirit shall return unto God who gave it." (Please, hold to this truth from start to finish of this book. Most theologians seem to overlook this truth when they deal with the status of life after death).

God, of course, could have chosen to cleanse the contaminated body of man. Jesus's blood is sufficient to cleanse even our fallen bodies. But for his own purpose, God elected to provide a new, glorified—a celestial—body. For whatever reason, God finds it more important to provide a new body than to wash and repurify an old one. The Bible tells us he is making all things anew, including the heavens and earth. We just observed in the previous paragraph that the "dust (body) shall return to the earth as it was." John says at Revelation 21:5a, "And he that sat upon the throne said, Behold, I make all things new."

In light of that thought, it does not take long for one to go from the question I used to ask myself as a young person to an appreciation I have gained through acquiring a better understanding of the reason behind God's judgment concerning the natural death of man. Once upon a time, the idea of death disturbed me greatly—that is, the fact that we had to live for a period of time and then die. With the perspective from which I viewed death, it would not have mattered too much if we were all living more than nine hundred years. The thought of life coming to an end at any point was both dreadful and fearful. It seemed to me that God was being insensitive and inconsiderate. I spent a portion of my life pondering the sure fact that my life was subject to be required of me at any given moment. It just seemed so unfair.

Today, as I look back upon that time of my life of constant fear and dread, I realize that God has blessed me with tremendous peace and contentment. If you are having problems following my notion of being blessed in knowing that it is a good thing to not have to spend eternity in the misery of sin, just think of how bad it would be to spend a thousand years in a state of real depression. If you happen to not get the point, then multiply that thousand by hundreds, which still would not come close to eternity! That is the blessing God's intervention bestows upon us concerning making the Tree of Life in the Garden of Eden unavailable to mankind.

Since coming to the conclusion that our being appointed to natural death is a blessing, I have been able to encourage many people over the years as I have counseled and consoled the bereaved, and I have conveyed this revelation to many from the pulpit and other places I have taught. I have observed that people are very much comforted when they get the revelation behind the reason for natural death. It eliminates the anger some people unwisely have toward God for allowing their loved ones to die. It is natural for us to feel that each person's life should belong to that individual. We tend to rest with the attitude that an individual is on this earth for his or her individual purpose. But that is not so. It is all about God.

The knowledge and the understanding of the cause and reason for natural death do not numb the dread and regret of losing a loved one or friend, but such knowledge and understanding make it much easier to accept their departure. Even if someone close to you was to go to an earthly place that could be likened to paradise and you were guaranteed to never see that person again in this life, there would probably be dread involved. You could learn that your loved one would experience nothing but peace and joy and happiness for the rest of his or her life, but there would likely still be some dread involved. If that person had been close to you, you would dread the idea of never being able to see or communicate with him or her again.

What I am suggesting is that dreading the departure of a friend or loved one is not likely to cease just because you gain an understanding—and, perhaps, an appreciation—of the fact that we do not have to reside eternally in these contaminated and corrupted bodies. Dreading the departure of people who mean much to us is common, whether they die or go to some other place that causes a permanent loss of contact. But at the same time, unless we are too selfish to care, we would be glad to know that the friend or loved one had gone to a place of paradise, no matter how much the person is missed. When we truly love someone, we do not wish to deny that person the peace and joy and happiness that await merely to satisfy our individual and selfish desires. Ultimately, our love for the person causes us to wish him or her well. If we truly understand the peace and joy that the departed Christian moves into, how can we be sad or have sorrow for that person? His or her departure should be a time of celebration, although it is likely to come with mixed emotions simply because we will miss the person's presence terribly.

Natural Death Lasts but a Moment

We have a tendency to fear what we do not understand. A lack of understanding natural death can certainly bring about much fear. I have encountered people who were not afraid to die but still had dread for one reason or another. There is nothing wrong with dreading certain things under certain circumstances. For instance, I have ministered to people in hospitals and residential care homes who sensed they had come to the end of their natural lives. Some were eager to depart because they saw themselves going to be with the Lord, and some were eager because they were very ill and did not see themselves getting any better. But some, I recall, dreaded immediate departure because there was someone they were not ready to leave behind. In other cases, I have ministered to people who were betwixt and between, so to speak. They felt they would immediately lift up their eyes in the presence of the Lord, but they had unfinished matters or desires that caused them to not be ready at that particular time. Those kinds of strong desires can cause one to have dread, but we must not confuse fear with dread. Having anxiety about dying because you are afraid of leaving here is caused by sheer fear.

What if someone feels he or she just might go to hell after death? What if someone feels there is no life after death? Let me address the first question before the second one. First, if one feels he or she might end up in hell, that means the person believes there is life after death. Therefore, remedying that fear is simple—by accepting the saving grace of Jesus Christ. But the person should not attempt to become saved for the expressed or intended purpose of escaping hell. Instead, he or she should immediately get to know Jesus and accept him because he is good and because the individual wants to embrace his cause and spend the rest of eternity with him. In short, to come to Jesus with the wrong motive does not work. People who do so find themselves among those who say they are Christians but whose lifestyles say the opposite.

Let me address the second question. If there is no life after death, it does not make sense to fear dying. How can one possibly fear what one considers to be absolutely nothing? If you are a person who does not believe life continues after death yet you fear dying, know that Satan is playing tricks on your mind big time. I would suggest that deep beneath that surface of skepticism lies confusion. You want to believe, but you are just not sure. If that sounds like you, I suggest that you immediately get with someone who can introduce you to the truth of the Bible as it pertains to eternal life through Jesus Christ. Again, it is not about blind faith. You need to learn about the Lord, and I pray you do it quickly.

I wish to share with you that when a Christian moves into eternity, there is no time span between death and resurrection. It is good for us to be reminded of this truth occasionally. When man's spirit returns to the Lord, we can declare that he went to heaven in the sense that God is in heaven. But wait a moment. That will put those who died in their sin in heaven as well. (As I have studied the meaning of heaven, I find it literally means "upward." Most of the time, "downward" refers to that which is of the earth—earthly.) But the good news is that because of the lack of a span of time between the two events, the saint and the sinner both return to the Lord. Those are not my words. We just read that truth at Ecclesiastes 12:7. To reiterate, there is no time span between natural death and resurrection. He who dies this minute moves out of the realm of time. Without the person experiencing any delay to any degree, he finds himself in the presence of God (as in the same moment, the twinkling of an eye, just as quickly as those who are alive and are changed at the last trump; see 1 Cor. 15:52). No measuring of time means "no downtime" to any extent. Therefore, within the moment that one passes from this life, he is resurrected in the life to come. Please keep that declaration in mind. Stay with me and you are sure to understand what I am saying.

The above reality holds the key to totally eliminating the Christian's fear of and intimidation by death. Death has no power over us. Natural death only puts us to sleep, and we wake up in a cognitive state in the presence of God at the first resurrection, which appears to the dead as taking place immediately upon dying. Only to the living does there appear to be a waiting period between death and the resurrection of the dead.

The Cause and Reason behind Spiritual Death

I stated earlier that I wish to cover two major discussions in this chapter. We just talked about natural death; let us now address spiritual death.

Spiritual death does not refer to the end of life. We find the following words declared at John 11:25–26: "Jesus said unto her, I am the resurrection, and the life: he that believeth in me, though he were dead, yet shall he live: and whosoever liveth and believeth in me shall never die. Believest thou this?" Observe that Martha, to whom Jesus is making the above address, first speaks of Lazarus's natural death, which the Lord referred to as having fallen asleep.

Though one dies a natural death, his spirit, which is the core of his being, never dies. And he shall be raised by Jesus on the day of resurrection. The difference between one who dies in Christ and one who dies without Christ is that he who is in Christ has an eternal relationship with God but he who is not has eternal torment and damnation. No man's spirit ever ceases to exist. Noteworthy are the words of the Lord, which say, "And fear not them which kill the body, but are not able to kill the soul: but rather fear him which is able to destroy both soul and body in hell" (Matt.

10:28). This verse is a reminder that even God does not infer or talk about destruction of the spirit of man. This, in my opinion, has to do with the fact the spirit of man comes directly from the eternal spirit of God, which cannot be destroyed. (The breath that God breathed into the nostrils of man is exactly that—the breath or wind or spirit of God.) And the breath of God is eternal, without exception.

I mentioned earlier that sin, prompted by disobedience, is the cause of spiritual death. Spiritual death is the end of quality life, which is composed of peace, joy, and righteousness. Our Lord God is the only source of those essentials and everything else that is good. In fact, James 1:17 says, "Every good gift and every perfect gift is from above, and cometh down from the Father of light." So, in the absence of access to those basic essentials of life, one is void of the essence that gives substance to life. For without peace, joy, and righteousness, one does not have what it takes to appreciate life as God has designed us to. Spiritual death means that a person's spirit man is without divine purpose—not having godly essence of life.

Romans 5:12 tells us that death came by way of sin. That was the beginning of what turned out to be spiritual and natural death for mankind. But just as disobedience by one man (Adam) led to death for all, by the obedience of one (Christ) shall many be made righteous (Rom. 5:19). Yes, we all died in Adam. King David says at Psalm 51:5, "Behold, I was shapen in iniquity; and in sin did my mother conceive me." But all believers are born again (a fresh, new start) in Christ. The act of Christ translates into eternal life for those who believe and receive Christ through an act of their will. Such a believer's spirit is no longer severed by sin. Although everyone, because of our natural birth, is born in sin, he who believes in the Lord Jesus obtains everlasting life.

Though we all died when Adam fell, we can be born again. In John 3, within the first several verses, Jesus has a discussion with a Pharisee named Nicodemus. There we learn that the dead in spirit can live again. In the discussion, Jesus says to Nicodemus in verse 3, "Verily, verily, I say unto thee, except a man be born again, he cannot see the kingdom of God." Being born again refers to recovering from or overcoming the first death (which took place in Adam). And he who overcomes the first death shall not see a second death. That is a very good thing, as seen in Revelation 21:8.

Prior to getting a better understanding of the principles and laws of God as it pertains to mankind, I wondered about being told I was guilty of something that happened long before I was born. But I learned that in Adam, God actually created all mankind. And in God's economy, everyone in Adam was equally guilty of disobeying the commandment to partake of the tree of the knowledge of good and evil. Yes, through Adam, we all died. But we shall discuss later the reality that the thing Satan thought would bring harm turned out for good for all who love God and put their trust in him.

It is hard to have this discussion without reiterating that sin is the very cause of man's spiritual death. What is sin? *Sin* simply means an intentional act or rebellion against God to any degree. Some Bible commentators and theologians suggest that the origin of sin is a mystery. I personally believe that sin originated with Lucifer's rebellion against God for, until then, no creature had ever acted against the will of God. Lucifer rebelled against God, and God changed his name to Satan. The devil was cast down from the presence of God. His separation from God caused him to possess a heart that is continually evil. God never gave him the opportunity to become reconciled.

Sin brings about death. Notice that death entered the world by sin. Death here refers to separation. Sin caused separation between God and man, and that kind of separation is spiritual death. Sin must not be viewed as an agent. Rather, sin is an act of one's will that is contrary to the will of God. One does not sin accidentally. That is why Romans 5:13 says, "For until the law sin was in the world: but sin is not imputed when there is no law." Here, Paul simply means that until God gave his laws, man had no law to break; therefore, God did not hold man accountable for his sin.

As sin pertains to mankind, the Bible tells us, "Wherefore, as by one man sin entered into the world, and death by sin; and so death passed upon all men, for that all have sinned" (Rom. 5:12). Satan was in the world prior to the fall of Adam. He was not a carrier of sin. Otherwise, sin would have come into the world the moment he entered. Satan was the instrument that influenced or tempted Adam to disobey God, but Adam is the instrument through which sin entered the world. Death of the natural body was brought on because God would not allow sinful man to live eternally spiritually dead. Adam is the instrument through which death was passed upon all men from both a spiritual and a natural standpoint.

In other words, by the divine appointment of God, Adam was the head and the representative of all his posterity that was to follow him. That is, all creation of mankind consisted in the loins of Adam. So, God, who had declared all his work of creation finished on the sixth day, was not about to open another mankind-creation factory, so to speak. Instead, he made a way that man could be reconciled (brought back) to God. And the shed blood of Jesus Christ is the way back.

Whereas the holiness, the righteousness, and the purity of God do not allow for sinners to comingle with Him, he has fixed it so that Christians can wear the cloak of the purity of Jesus Christ in this world, which we commonly refer to as imputed righteousness. Further, God has made provisions for resurrected saints to put on incorruptible, immortal bodies. The difference in being clothed with the righteousness of Christ in this life and being clothed with an incorruptible body at resurrection is that our corruptible body still exists on this side of death but the new, resurrected body will not be subject to any form or any degree of sin, period.

The new, resurrected body is also called a spiritual body or glorified body. Paul addresses the spiritual body at 1 Corinthians 15:44. He speaks of a body that will be composed of matter yet will not depend on natural productions or physical substances for its sustainability. However, it will still be one's dwelling place in the same manner as the Lord Jesus's earthly tabernacle was his dwelling place while on the earth. Listen to the words of the apostle: "It is sown a natural body; it is raised a spiritual body." There is such thing as a natural body, and there is such thing as a spiritual body. They are both material bodies.

Chapter Two

Life and Its Cause

Definition of the Term Life

Most word dictionaries will give you a pictorial definition of the word *life*. It can be defined in many ways, but we are primarily concerned with the life of mankind. I, however, describe natural life as a cluster of organismic matter joined together, and in a state characterized by the capacity for metabolism, growth, and reaction to stimuli and reproduction. I wish to discuss mainly the human life in this chapter. I wish to discuss it from the standpoint of one's three major components being united in order for one to be physically alive. I said earlier that man is tripartite in that he is spirit, body, and soul.

The natural human body is forever dying; this has been the case since the fall of man. Therefore, it is not uncommon to find bodies all about us that are malfunctioning in one way or another. The natural human body was neither designed nor intended to deteriorate; it deteriorates because it has been denied access to the Tree of Life. (The Bible puts hardly any emphasis on saving the natural human body. All things shall be made anew. Jesus did not die to save our contaminated bodies.) But as long as a human body resembles that described in the above definitions of a living body, it reflects natural life. That means it is functioning somewhat as it was designed to function.

Let us not forget that there is no such thing as the human's spirit ceasing to exist. Even when it sleeps, it is still alive. Lazarus was asleep, but his spirit was still alive. Remember, the human spirit is the eternal breath of the eternal God.

When we speak of spiritual life, we refer to the spirit's functioning as it was designed to function, including the fact that it is at the time occupying a body. You were designed to have communion with God. Of course, the opposite of that is that when the spirit is not functioning as it is meant to function, it is what we call dead (separated from God). The people who go to hell will be ever so alive and will be housed in bodies, but they will not have the essence of human life. Listen to Revelation 21:8: "But the fearful, and unbelievers, and whoremongers, and sorcerers, and idolaters, and all liars, shall have their part in the lake which burneth with fire and brimstone: which is the second death." God calls this state the "second death," which is the final (the eternal) state of those who remain spiritually dead. They will never cease to exist. But if they physically die while they are spiritually dead, they will never again have the opportunity to be with God.

"And as it is appointed unto man once to die, but after this the judgment" (Heb. 9:27). This verse speaks only of spiritual death. One only needs to read the next verse to grasp this truth: "So Christ was once offered to bear the sins of many; and unto them that look for him shall he appear the second time without sin unto salvation." Observe the comparison made here. The word *once* in verse 27, contrasted with the word *once* in verse 28, implies a condition of absoluteness. The Bible tells us that Jesus is not to be offered up a second or third time. Thus, in light of that truth, natural death is not considered in verse 27. We have plenty of biblical and nonbiblical characters alike who have died natural deaths more than once. And from that reality alone, we can conclude that the clause "it is appointed unto man *once* to die" does not address natural death. Further proof lies within verse 8 of Revelation 21, which discusses the second death. Yet the residents of hell will be materially whole and completely animated.

It is not proper to accept that there can be a second spiritual death without overcoming the first one. I am not aware of the Bible clearly stating at what point those who shall die the second death overcame the first death. But it is obvious one cannot die without first being alive. That is to say, I wish to not go on a so-called rabbit trail in an attempt to explain how a sinner becomes alive in order to experience a second death. It is possible that John was referring to a second judgment by God concerning separation from him. But somewhere between an unbeliever's birth and when he stands before the Lord for final judgment, his spirit has to become quickened in order for him to experience a second death. We know that the second death refers to eternal separation from God, and during that eternal separation the subject shall experience eternal torment. That much is clear.

Simply put, true life exists only when one is in communion and fellowship with our Creator. Apart from Him, we do not serve God's purpose as human beings. The only reason one might think he has life apart from Jesus Christ is that he is deceived by the master deceiver.

Life Must Consist in Real Substance

By definition, one is alive naturally when the spirit, body, and soul are united. (That is another truth we must hold to in this discussion.) Having three-part union is the minimum requirement to possess natural life. Without a spirit, there can be no soul, and without a soul, the body does not function.

Man is not designed or constructed in a manner that will permit him to live without a desire to worship and commune with God. What man does all too often is try to substitute other things for God. He even turns and looks to himself in some instances. But he shall get no satisfaction apart from God, no matter how hard he tries. Jesus is the only answer. Anyone in such a state remains most miserable. The intended purpose is not being met. Again, such a state is called dead (spiritually).

The unfortunate souls that end up in hell will not be void of life as a result of the pains of the fire and brimstone, though the pains will be difficult. The pains may be almost unbearable, but pain itself does not void one of life. It is the lack of the substance of life that makes for spiritual death. I can imagine Satan will be too busy gnashing his own teeth from his own pains to go about hell trying to further deceive any of the residents. Cognizance in its full measure will set in, and those unfortunate souls will come to their senses, as did the rich man in the story of Lazarus the beggar. They will realize their lives serve no purpose and offer no pleasant substance. The rich man in the story of Lazarus at Luke 16:19–31 was no longer preoccupied with earthly possessions and influence, so my thought is that the devil had no interest in trying to deceive him any longer.

We have associated being cognizant of our existence with true life for so long that we think of the cognizance itself as real life for the most part. Let us not forget that one has to possess and, in fact, exercise the ability to function as he is designed in order to have life in the true sense of the word.

If spiritual death for Adam meant that he lost the relationship between God and himself, then *spiritual life* refers to a reestablished relationship with the Lord that comes when one is born again. At Acts 17:28, referring to the Lord, the following words are recorded: "For in him we live, and move, and have our being; as certain also of your own poets have said, For we are also his offspring." Well, to live, move, and have our being requires one to become reconnected to the spirit of God. Such real substance is not hinged or connected to any other condition or circumstance. You may be in the poorest of health or abandoned by all of society, but if you are born again, you have real substance of life. Quite alive was the beggar Lazarus even while in this world. He may have seen many hungry days in his short earthly life, but that could never take away his substance of life. As a believer, his hope was in eternal life, and the same applies to each of us today. We all need to come to an understanding that only a spiritual connection with the Lord God can bring about real life substance.

MEANING OF NATURAL LIFE

You can connect a person to what we commonly call a life-support unit and keep the body alive for years. We consider that to be alive. But in many cases, the bodies are being totally manipulated artificially. Such a condition doest not meet the biblical definition of a living person. The truth of the matter is that I do not know where the line is drawn. That is to say, at some point the spirit leaves that body, but I dare not try to pinpoint the exact moment. We now have the ability to keep a corpse metabolizing as if a soul were still present. That I understand—as long as you keep the blood circulating so as to distribute oxygen and foodstuff and to eliminate carbon dioxide and waste matter, a lifeless body will continue to metabolize and mimic a normal body.

The physical or natural aspect of human life can be described as that possessed by one who is united in body, spirit, and soul. In such state, one has the necessary vitality to be distinguished from the dead. That is natural life in a nutshell. And if any one of the three components or entities is removed, natural life is interrupted. Remember that Genesis 2:7 tells us "man became a living soul." It happened when, and not before, God breathed the breath of life into the nostrils of the body of man. In most of the arguments I have studied either for or against "soul-sleeping," it seems that the fact that man is not designed to be aware of his existence apart from the union of his major three components is overlooked.

We have billions of human souls in the world today who have natural lives. Many of them also live (naturally), move, and have their being. But Acts 17:28 addresses or reflects on people who have those qualities in Christ Jesus. Natural life does not in itself contain the substance of spiritual life. Natural life draws its substance from natural things, and the substance of those natural things feeds only the flesh or carnality of the natural man. And that is the state we sometimes refer to as the "walking dead." People who are deceived into thinking they are experiencing life with substance are simply ensnared by the master deceiver, Satan. They cannot miss what they have never known. For instance, a person who is born blind in the natural and remains blind will never know he is blind unless someone tells him. He will never miss what he does not know exists. In like manner, the spiritually blind do not actually know they are blind. In order to change, the Holy Spirit has to give them the grace to accept by faith the new birth.

MEANING OF SPIRITUAL LIFE

I wish to state up front that there is a major difference between spiritual life and one's spirit in the context of this discussion. Let us not forget that the spirit of each human being is eternal in all cases. It has been pointed out that the spirit never ceases to exist. But when it is separated from whence it came (God), it ceases to function in the purpose for which it exists. The term *spiritual life*, from a biblical perspective, refers to the status of one's spirit. By now, if not before, we understand that he who is born again has spiritual life, and even the damned have everlasting spirits.

We have inherent citizenship of both the natural and the spiritual worlds. That makes us different from all other beings. Keep in mind that God created and suited us to occupy this natural world, yet he designed us so we could commune in the spirit world in which he lives. We should always take into account the duality of our citizenship when we are considering the life of the dead. We are not designed to function in the spirit world apart from the natural world, nor are we designed to function in the natural world apart from the spirit world. God has given us this duality for a specific purpose. I know that some of us like to think of heaven as a big supernatural place trillions of miles somewhere up yonder. However, any way one says it, our heaven shall be in the new earth.

You see, because of our design and purpose, God created the natural, even our bodies, for man's convenience in realizing the joy he set before us in this world. The animal kingdom can find joy and comfort in the natural. He has given us silver and gold and all kinds of natural beauty. He has given us everything necessary to comfort and bring pleasure to the natural man. That is why it is quite okay to gather and enjoy things of the natural. But we should never put them on the same plane as our joy of the Lord. He has given us special emotions that stimulate and gratify our natural senses. God wants you to embrace what he has given you, but you should keep it in proper perspective. He says to us at Matthew 6:33, "But seek ye first the kingdom of God, and his righteousness; and all these things shall be added unto you." We are not to put anything or anyone on the high plane that should be reserved for our love toward God. Hopefully, by now you can plainly grasp what I am trying to say. God has given the earth to the children of man. He wants you us to enjoy and be comfortable in it.

But God put his spirit in man for his own joy and delight. God's spirit, which is the core of our being, is for his purpose, not ours. Had he not wanted us for the joy and delight of Himself, perhaps we would have been odd-looking creatures on this earth with no more spirit than the ape, monkey, cat, or dog, which has none. But it was God's delight to create us in his image and after his own likeness. With this truth in mind, it should not be difficult for one to see and understand that man's design does not lend itself toward his functioning apart from a body.

God did not create and leave us, as he did other earthly creatures. He put the wind of the spirit of God into us, making us into the image and likeness of the Godhead (*Elohim*). I cannot overstate the truth that God created us to commune and fellowship with him. It is called worship. And at John 4:23–24, we are told, "But the hour cometh, and now is, when the true worshippers shall worship the Father in spirit and in truth: for the father seeketh such to worship him. God is a Spirit: and they that worship him must worship him in spirit and in truth." The physical and material aspect of our being is gathered from the natural resources, but our worship is done in spirit and truth. Our nice temples and other beautiful surroundings do not make for worship. Our spirits must touch and agree with the spirit of God.

Let us all be careful not to settle for the generic definition that confines life to creatures possessing the vitality that distinguishes them from inanimate objects. The generic definition of *life* does not properly represent us. It includes plants and animals. God said to the Israelites, "I call heaven and earth to record this day against you, that I have set before you life and death, blessing and cursing: therefore choose life, that both thou and thy seed may live" (Deut. 30:19). In that particular instance, natural life was the focus, but in this new dispensation, eternal life is the focus. God used the natural in the days of the Old Testament to steer us in the direction of the New Testament. And this does not mean we are to now disregard the Old Testament, as some seem to think. Those who believed the promise that was to come also have hope of eternal life. They too were blessed with the grace of God.

Do not settle for the lies from Satan that try to lead you to believe that you have life just because you have the necessary vitality that grants you the ability to function in your natural body. We were designed and constructed for much more than mere earthly existence. Satan is a master at deceptive appeasement. He will do all he can to cause you to become numbed to that inward longing to be reconnected to the spirit of God. But I dare anyone to make that thrust and invite the Lord Jesus Christ into his or her heart—to become born again. The person's eyes will come open to the truth of life, and he or she will be able to see right through the lies of the devil.

We have people whose inward spirits are longing for something special, and they cannot figure out what exactly they are longing for at that moment. Naturally, Satan is the perpetrator behind such confusion. It reminds me of someone having a taste for a certain food and being unable to determine what food is wanted. On the other hand, people sometimes have itches but cannot find the exact spot. They just start scratching. In like manner, people know in their spirits that something else is desired but cannot quite determine what is missing. This causes some to experiment with various religions, with drugs, with other immoralities; some heap up wealth, and the list goes on. They are searching for that itch but are scratching in the wrong places. So, the itch goes on, and so does the attempt to scratch it.

The Bible, in the book of Ecclesiastes, gives what I consider to be the best illustration of someone trying to fill that inward longing apart from communion and fellowship with God. But first let us go to the book of Second Chronicles. In Chapter 1, verses 11 and 12, we find the following words: "And God said to Solomon, Because this was in thine heart, and thou hast not asked riches, wealth, or honour, nor the life of thine enemies, neither yet has asked long life; but hast asked wisdom and knowledge for thyself, that thou mayest judge my people, over whom I have made thee king: Wisdom and knowledge is granted unto thee; and I will give thee riches, and wealth, and honour, such as none of the kings have had that have been before thee, neither shall there any after thee have the like."

If you turn to the book of Ecclesiastes, you will find that Solomon got caught up in his wealth and riches. Despite all the wisdom he possessed, he began to live a life outside the will and ways of God, and he found himself without important life substance. In Chapter 1, Solomon said he gave his heart to seek and search out wisdom concerning all things that are done under heaven. Verse 14 says, "I have seen all the works that are done under the sun; and, behold, all is vanity and vexation of spirit." As you read forward, you find that Solomon succeeded in accomplishing many difficult tasks.

Looking farther at verses 16–18 of Chapter One, Solomon says, "I communed with mine own heart, saying, Lo, I am come to great estate, and have gotten more wisdom than all they that have been before me in Jerusalem: yea, my heart had great experience of wisdom and knowledge. And I gave my heart to know wisdom, and to know madness and folly: I perceived that this also is vexation of spirit. For in much wisdom is much grief: and he that increaseth knowledge increaseth sorrow." It is well stated in those few verses above. But take time to read the whole story. It plainly shows that real life substance consists not in the abundance of things or any other act of man apart from having communion and fellowship with God.

Solomon, in his old age, came to the proper conclusion. Before coming to his senses, he had taken on seven hundred wives—princesses—and three hundred concubines. The Bible tells us, "His wives turned away his heart after other gods: and his heart was not perfect with the Lord his God, as was the heart of David his father" (1 Kings 11:3–4). But thanks be to God, Solomon finally came to himself and realized he was scratching in all the wrong places in an attempt to calm that itch. Ecclesiastes 12:13 reveals that the preacher has come to a proper understanding of life's purpose. He says, "Let us hear the conclusion of the whole matter: Fear God, and keep his commandments: for this is the whole duty of man." Only at the point of realizing that God is our only source of true life will we come to the conclusion that Solomon reached. It is at that point that one understands that life is not really worth living outside of a relationship and without communion and fellowship with God. There is no other way to experience real spiritual life.

Meaning of Life More Abundantly

The Bible makes quite plain the truth that Satan came into the garden and beguiled Eve. Adam joined Eve in the act of disobedience, and it caused him to lose the wonderful life God had bestowed upon him. And thus, many years later, Jesus Christ is manifest and preaches the way back to true life. He says at John 10:10, "The thief cometh not, but for to steal, and to kill, and to destroy: I am come that they might have life, and that they might have it more abundantly." Life always points to God. It is a gift from God. James says that all good and perfect gifts come from him (James 1:17). But at John 10:10, Jesus says that he has come that we might have life *more abundantly*.

The first question that springs forth is perhaps, "More abundantly than what?" or "In what way might life be more abundant?" If all gifts from God are perfect (and they are) and if life is a gift from God (and it is), how can perfection be increased or improved upon? Would not life more abundantly suggest perfection is being raised to a higher level? If so, that would definitely be indicative of imperfection. But it is not like that by any means.

The phrase "more abundantly" does not diminish perfection. For example, if you were to mint a 100 percent pure, flawless silver dime and give it to your best friend today, it would be a flawless or perfect gift. And if tomorrow you were to mint a 100 percent pure, flawless silver dollar to give to the same friend, what would be the difference in perfection? I submit that neither one would bear perfection more than the other, but there would be quite a difference in value and in denomination. Obviously, the silver dollar would be more abundant. Though they are both perfect, one would be preferred over the other.

Likewise, "life more abundantly" does not refer to improved perfection but rather to plain "increase." Life in the Garden of Eden was glorious and wonderful in every respect (and there is room to be much more descriptive, but not this time). Just think of yourself living in a garden designed and planted by God Himself, without the assistance of any creature. Think of the incomprehensible perfection, the fragrance, the beauty, and the atmosphere. I can imagine the morning chirping of the birds being a heavenly melody to the ears and hearts of the inhabitants. What a garden!

For the children of Israel in the Old Testament setting, life was wonderful in comparison to that of the rest of the world. But at John 10:10, Jesus declares that he has come to bring life and to bring it with greater essence than man had ever known. He declares a gracious and glorious life of the height, depth, and width that shall perhaps constitute our spending eternity exploring and experiencing it without end. That is life, my friend. The good news is that we do not have to wait until the resurrection to begin enjoying abundant life; it is the life offered us today. Had Jesus not come, we would have no life. We find recorded at John 3:36: "He that believeth on the Son hath everlasting life: and he that believeth not the Son shall not see life; but the wrath of God abideth on him." You might not have begun to comprehend the infinite life you possess in Christ at this moment, but if you are born of the spirit of God, you have it without measure.

The full measure of "life more abundantly" is realized without interruption once you put on immortality. It will happen because there will be no hint of evil or wickedness. There will be no opposition to the will of God. You will have an eternity of real utopianism. It often comes to my attention how Genesis tells us that in the cool of the day the voice of the Lord came walking through the garden and called out to Adam (Gen. 3:8–9). It is believed that God visited Adam and Eve often. But as I think on that passage, I go farther to Revelation 21:3. There, I am reminded of the truth that God shall not merely visit man in the cool of the day; he shall dwell with man and man with him. This means a continual presence. God will not be stopping by looking for us. We will be his eternal tabernacle without interruption. Such an awesome presence of God is life more abundantly.

A Deeper and Richer Life

Life in this world can pass you by so rapidly that you might feel that you have hardly had any time between birth and growing old. Some people spend lots of time focusing and dwelling on the fact that they have to die someday. We all need to go ahead and accept the facts that death is inevitable and that life in this land is short. James 4:12 says, "Whereas ye know not what shall be on the morrow. For what is your life? It is even a vapour, that appeareth for a little time, and then vanisheth away." But when you have eternal life, you should begin to think in terms of natural death being merely the threshold to everlasting bliss! Please do not look upon death as your arch enemy.

The shortness of life should have no bearing on the quality of life—the joy and the peace and the righteousness in Christ. As a child of God, you should sense richness and joy in the Lord daily. And when we take into account all God has done to bring us back to Himself and all he promises us throughout eternity, it should become impossible to view death as our enemy. I have heard of saints who display an attitude in reference to death that says, "Bring it on!" They have no problem with dying.

Being an inheritor of eternal life, whatever adversities come your way, you need to be able to say, with conviction, "This too shall pass." Richness or any good quality of life is not realized through the abundance of things. Such comes through a proper attitude concerning life in Christ. We can put our trust in Christ and leave it there only when we realize that living in this world shall be brief at most and that God has already promised he will never forsake us or leave us alone (Heb. 13:5). So, what thing or circumstance has the power to rob you of your righteousness, peace, and joy in the Holy Spirit? The answer is none! Only you have the power to rob yourself.

Remember that the generic definition of *life* confines it to creatures possessing the vitality that distinguishes them from inanimate objects. Do not settle for the lies from Satan that try to lead you to believe a person has true life just because he has the necessary vitality that grants the ability to function in his natural body. You are designed and constructed for much more than mere earthly existence. You are designed and constructed for the purpose of being a vital companion with God as well as with your fellow men.

Reserved for every believer is a deeper and richer meaning in life. We must make attitude adjustments accordingly. That is to say, we must make conscious efforts to understand and embrace the deep meaning of life. The apostle Paul renders a beautiful example of proper attitude at Philippians 1:21, where he says, "For me to live is Christ, and to die is gain." Paul had come to the conclusion that it was Christ all the way. The point is that while he was alive on earth, he belonged to Christ. When the time came to die, he would do so in Christ and the troubles of this world would be over for him. That would be a gain because he would go directly to the presence of Christ. Thus, it would be a win-win situation.

God allows us to stay here for the purpose of helping him to advance his kingdom. But when he allows us to depart, that means we go from labor to reward—from bearing our crosses of this life to wearing our crowns of eternal life. Paul very well understood this reality and longed to be with the Lord.

The deep meaning of life surfaces when one stops and considers the true meaning of his living. As Rick Warren so eloquently put it, "It is not about any one of us." We were created for and still exist for God's purpose. Becoming reconnected to God does not happen just because one decides he wants to be with him. Our Bible tells us, "But God commendeth his love toward us, in that, while we were yet sinners, Christ died for us" (Rom. 5:8). Also, "For ye are bought with a price: therefore glorify God in your body and in your spirit, which are God's." There is no account of man's negotiating with God concerning reconciliation. It has pleased God to buy us back for his own purpose, and we ought to be glad and grateful that God is so mindful of us. We are not talking about some outstanding and influential businessman. We are talking about the eternal God of all creation being unbelievably mindful of us! Paul says at Philippians 4:8, "Finally, brethren, whatsoever things are true, whatsoever things are honest, whatsoever things are just, whatsoever things are pure, whatsoever things are lovely, whatsoever things are of good report; if there be any virtue, and if there be any praise, think on these things." The price for us is paid for by the precious blood of Jesus Christ. He wants to bring everyone back to a state of true life, and he offers us life even more abundantly.

As we think on those virtuous things God has done for us, even buying us back with the blood of himself in the person of his son Jesus, a deeper meaning of life comes to the forefront. There is great joy in realizing that the God we are talking about chose us. We are his elect. When we stop and think on the things that Paul points out at Philippians 4:8, we too can take on the attitude Paul exemplified when he said, "Not that I speak in respect of want: for I have learned, in whatsoever state I am, therewith to be content. I know both how to be abased, and I know how to abound: every where and in all things I am instructed both to be full and to be hungry, both to abound and to suffer need. I can do all things through Christ which strengtheneth me" (Phil. 4:12–13). We need to allow contentment to flow according to our attitudes. Thus, if we take on an attitude of great gratitude, we too can be content in whatever state we find ourselves. Even during a time of weeping over that which is grievous, we need not be moved. Psalm 30:5 says, "For his anger endureth but a moment; in his favor is life: *weeping may endure for a night, but joy cometh in the morning*" (emphasis added). In other words, weeping too will pass. Yet it is not the weeping that matters. What does matter is our attitude toward the event or circumstance that triggered the weeping.

It was only a short time ago that I sat with the pastor of one of our churches and consoled him following the death of his oldest daughter. Just two months earlier, he had lost a son. He is a professional individual and group counselor who has consoled many, and it was necessary for me to use the approach he uses when counseling and consoling others. I had sensed that he was extremely grieved over the loss of his daughter. We sat for slightly more than an hour, and all of a sudden there appeared to be a breakthrough. Perhaps I had said nothing that the preacher had not said to others over and over again, but at times our knowledge and convictions of certain things need to be reinforced through someone else. There will come a time when someone else can comfort you with words you already know and understand very well.

As you journey through this life, always remember your relationship with the God of all creation. Never forget that he has purposed to be with you every step of the way. It will make a major difference when you take into account such truths as these: (1) "And I know that all things work together for good to them that love God, to them who are the called according to his purpose" (Rom. 8:28); (2) "These things I have spoken unto you, that in me ye might have peace. In the world ye shall tribulation: *but be of good cheer; I have overcome the world*" (John 16:33; emphasis added). There are many uplifting passages of Scripture that will strengthen you and provide fuel for this journey through life, giving you a deeper and richer meaning of life as you go. Scripture raises the question: "For what shall it profit a man, if he shall gain the whole world, and lose his own soul? Or what shall a man give in exchange for his soul?" (Mark 8:36–37). The satisfaction of knowing that when this life is over you will be departing to be eternally with the giver and sustainer of life is the greatest comfort and the richest substance one can experience in this life. And in order for that truth to remain before us, without the "accuser" succeeding in causing our faith to waver concerning these matters, we must strive to walk circumspectly before the Lord. Do not strive for the purpose of touching God's hand. Out of love for Him, strive for the purpose of touching his heart.

CHAPTER THREE

Everyone Is Touched by Death

FACE THE FACTS OF DEATH

The Bible lets us know that death has been passed upon all men: "Wherefore, as by one man sin entered into the world, and death by sin; and so death passed upon all men, for that all have sinned" (Rom. 5:12). In light of this, everyone is touched by the death of someone else. The question is, are you prepared to accept the death of everyone who is close to you?

Most of us spend years preparing for careers, but one of the most common things in life seems to draw only minimum attention from us until it actually strikes. Yes, I am talking about death. Many take a similar approach to learning effective parenting, but I will not discuss that issue in this book. We attend schools of various types. We undergo technical training, and we attend seminars and receive on-the-job training. But it seems that most teaching and training institutions, churches included, fail to encourage the people to prepare for the deaths of their loved ones and friends. For the most part, churches do teach individuals to prepare for life after death. But it is time for everyone to get ready and stay ready for death. It is coming your way someday. Of equal importance, it is time that we understand what actually happens to our loved ones and friends immediately upon departure from this life when they die in Christ.

Some people have been led to believe that they will rush death by discussing it. That is not true. Death comes whether you discuss it or not.

It is very helpful for both the living and the dying to have already come to a point of acceptance of death. I have observed that most patients I have encountered thus far who have received formal counseling pertaining to the end of life are more apt to embrace the idea of their coming departure than those who have not been counseled. Likewise, the family members who have received good counseling are much better prepared to release their dying loved ones.

Chances are that not only have you been touched by death, but you are likely to keep being touched until your time comes. So what are you supposed to do? Ignoring the matter does not make it better; however, it has been known to make matters worse. Family members and whoever will be directly affected by the death of a particular person should come together and discuss the issue of dying. It is not a matter of whether you will be touched. The questions are about when and how well you will be prepared. Good preparation can make a lot of difference. I directed a funeral for a young lady recently, and it went very smoothly. My wife and I spent the night preceding the day of the funeral with the young lady's parents, and I had the opportunity to share with the father the essence of my convictions as recorded in this book. I sensed the immediate comfort that came to him.

The family and friends did not display a lot of sadness. During the funeral service, the family, for the most part, did not display much emotion. It was a celebration in the true sense of the word. In addition to the fact that the young lady had been saved, she had seen to it that all necessary arrangements would be in order. Her departure was not complicated with the burden of her family's having to figure out how to settle her estate or get her bills paid. She had taken care of all of that.

Considering the reality of the life of the dead, in which you shall be included, makes one more apt to prepare for the dying day. I cannot help but often think of the life and death of the apostle Paul when I am talking or simply reflecting on the closure on this side of life. For instance, when he came to the end of life on this side of the threshold of eternal glory, he said, "For I am now ready to be offered, and the time of my departure is at hand. I have fought a good fight, I have finished my course, I have kept the faith: Henceforth there is laid up for me a crown of righteousness, which the Lord, the righteous judge, shall give me at that day and not to me only, but unto all them also that love his appearing" (2 Tim. 4:6–8). Many times had God delivered Paul from the jaws of death. That was because God had further work for Paul to do. But when he came to the end of his journey, he was ready to be offered up. It was not the intelligence of Paul that caused him to be ready to be offered up. It was the grace of God that provided him such delight. Paul merely accepted the grace that God offers to all believers.

Many believers live their lives boasting of their eternal salvation and the fact that they can hardly wait to see Jesus face to face. At the same time, many of them are plagued by the thought that something could happen at any moment that would result in their death. But meanwhile, they sound like they are eager to go be with the Lord. It is the fear of what they do not know—what they do not understand—that makes them afraid. That is why it is so necessary to get a real understanding of death and the life of the dead. The apostle Paul had understanding.

You are encouraged to make a special effort to sit down with family members and anyone else who will be directly affected by your death to begin an earnest dialogue concerning the inevitable deaths of one another. If you are born again, encourage your loved ones to understand how precious it is in the sight of God when you cross the threshold from mortality to immortality. Psalm 116:15 tells us, "Precious in the sight of the Lord is the death of his saints." We must put on immortality in order to be a lively stone in the eternal tabernacle of God, as mentioned in Revelation 21. We must all be changed in order to be a part of that new tabernacle. Thus, unless you live until Jesus returns, you will have to die in order to qualify to spend eternity with him. In fact, if you live to see the rapture, you will still die in that you will become separated from your mortal body.

For many years I have arranged for a certain poem to be read each Resurrection Sunday. It is "Death Meets His Master" by Elwood McQuaid. It is a powerful poem that is well worth reading. The copy I have on file was published by Moody in March 1986. It paints a wonderful picture of death encountering the Lord Jesus. The poem personifies death as King Death, and it personifies time as Father Time. It gives a picture of King Death having heard the rumor that Jesus said he would go into the grave but would rise on the third day, which was a put-down to King Death. So he had stopped attending to the death of others and was sitting around the tomb to bear witness to Jesus's not being raised on the third day.

As Father Time came by to tuck away darkness and make way for the sun to shine that morning, he came across King Death and had a brief dialogue with him. The bottom line was that King Death boasted that Jesus would not be allowed to undo the death hold he had put on him.

Father Time attested to the fact that he had seen death put many bodies down that were still down.

King Death was prepared to watch over the Lord's grave for only three days. After that, it would be necessary for him to return to his usual business. Thus, on the second day, he let Father Time know that he would not be there when Father Time came by on the third day. He boasted that he had to get back to spreading grief and sorrow across the land.

The poem goes on to depict the resurrection of Jesus early that Sunday morning while King Death sits by the tomb. The poem tells that when Father Time came by that morning, he found Death quivering on the ground, full of fright and agony. Death explained to Father Time what had happened early that morning. Death said that all of a sudden, the whole world began to reel and roll. He said the stone that sealed the tomb seemed to have removed itself from the door and skipped down the hill.

Death gave the whole story to Father Time. He explained how awesome Jesus looked as he stood at the door where the stone had rolled away. He mentioned that Jesus did not say a word; he just stood there, and speaking of himself, Death said he became very tired and weak. And Death told Father Time that Jesus got a hold on him, threw him down, and put his foot on his neck. And then Jesus took his keys and his crown.

The poem closes with Father Time coming across Death another time much later somewhere else. Father Time greeted Death, saying something to the effect of "It is good seeing you again." Father Time inquired as to Death's fate, and Death responded, "I'm just a lowly servant now. There is little time to roam. I just push open this old gate and help the saints get home!" That is a true picture of what death means to those of us who are born of the spirit of God.

AFFECTED WITHOUT KNOWING IT

I can recall being concerned and very dreadful of the thought of death from my early childhood. I was not so much concerned about facing my personal fate of death in those earlier years. It seemed that the odds of my living a long time were in my favor. But I agonized over the thought of someday having to die. Like the average youngster, I felt as if I would live forever on one hand, but on the other hand I knew I still had to die. I had a grandmother (my mother's mother) of whom I was most fond. She was my best friend. I did not know how to classify her as my best friend during my early childhood days, but later in life, as I looked back on our closeness, I could see that she was my very best friend, bar none. I called my grandmother Momma.

During her early childhood, Momma was stricken with malaria. She told me that in a rush to get well and back to school faster, not knowing better, she got out of the bed, found the medicine the doctor had prescribed for her, and consumed it all in one dose. Needless to say, she became worse, near death, and the side effect caused her to be ill for the rest of her life. Thus, she was ill the whole time I knew her. She was also what is commonly called legally blind.

As a little child, I became Momma's seeing-eye guide when we would go downtown and other places while the rest of the family was at work. Also, I loved to scratch her head with a comb and style her soft and silky hair from time to time. I grew up sitting at her feet and listening to stories, many of which had been handed down to her. Through that process, I became closely attached to Momma over the years, even closer than to my mother. Our special friendship, plus the fact that it appeared she would die soon rather than later, caused me to be concerned about her likely soon departure from this life. The thought itself created dread that I interpreted as fear.

I went into the military as a college dropout. From that point onward, I did not see Momma very often. Three and a half years later, she passed away. To that point, I had experienced a tremendous fear and dread of losing my grandmother during those years of my absence. I had served a three-year tour in West Germany and was serving at Fort Hood, Texas, when I got the call that Momma had died. During my absence, I had convinced myself that life would be most difficult to live if Momma died while I was away. In short, I wanted to spend more time with her.

I would describe and discuss the special friendship I had with my grandmother with whomever would listen. My girlfriend there in Texas knew how close Momma and I were. And on December 16, 1966—the day the telephone call came—the fear and dread I had had all those years turned into a sea of peace and calmness. My grandmother had lived a Christian life second to none I have witnessed even to this day. As I took into account all that I had heard about Christian believers going to heaven, I knew everything had to be all right for Momma. When I shared the news with my girlfriend, she began to weep. Though I was not aware of making the statement at the time, my girlfriend shared with others what my response was when I observed her weeping after the news of Momma's death. She said my response was, "Why are you crying? She was my grandmother."

From the day of Momma's death to the day of my mother's death, approximately thirty years later, I considered myself as being at peace with the death of my mother and grandmother. In fact, three months following the death of my mother, my youngest brother died from complications brought on by maltreatment of a doctor. The following year, my youngest sister died from an accidental puncturing of her stomach, also done by a doctor, but this was not determined until it was too late. And the next year, we lost the second oldest of my brothers because of a blood clot in one of his lungs. I thought I was at peace with all of those deaths. As far as I knew, I had not grieved any of the five deaths of my immediate family members. I thought I was gifted with the magic to just turn off the switch and close the curtains to those who become deceased.

As a minister of the gospel, I eulogized and preached the funerals of family members, including my mother. There did not appear to be any grief or unusual emotions present during either the preparation or the delivery of the eulogies and sermons. But when my brother Robert died, the last immediate family member we have lost to this point, I headed back home for his funeral. I picked up a rental car at the airport and drove it to my hometown. As I entered the outskirts of town and saw all the familiar sites and the changed landscape, memories of the past set in, and I began reminiscing of things pertaining to my early childhood. It seemed like memories of my whole childhood crossed my mind. Things flashed before me perhaps as rapidly as one dreams while sleeping. The process awakened memories that stirred my emotions considerably. Before I realized what was happening, I began weeping uncontrollably. I wept for seemingly a long time. And once I finished, it seemed the weeping had done me more good than any medicine could have done. Heaviness within, that I had not been conscious of bearing, lifted. Suddenly, my soul felt washed.

Despite studying psychology and other aspects of human behavior over the years, I had not recognized the grief that I was bottling up inside, so to speak. But later, as I began to reflect on the experience I had that day as I entered my hometown, it began to come together. Being such a close-knit family as we are, why would I ever think that the loss of a family member would not grieve me? My conclusion is that I just buried or covered it up. Like a volcano, grief had been brewing inside me since the death of Momma, and the reminiscing caused the eruption. But the rupture was a good thing.

Today, when I attempt to console bereaved people, I suggest to them that it is okay to grieve; it is okay to weep. It is okay to show emotions. But it is not okay to try to bury your feelings, nor is it okay to allow grief to linger too long. I know of cases where people have lost loved ones and continue moaning and lamenting for years. That is perhaps worse than my behavior following the loss of my family members. But in short, it is neither good to bury it nor to allow it to linger for a long period of your life.

Fortunately, each family member we have lost professed to being a born-again believer. I found consolation in the idea that they were Christians. But that had not eradicated or blotted out the truth that I had lost people who were dear to me and I would never see them again in this life. From the end of 1966 to the middle of 1997, I was suffering from a form of grief and was not aware of the cause of the problem. Every time it would begin to surface, I would find myself packing it down and putting it under my feet, seeing that I could not stop it from happening. So please, do not ever try to do as I did. At the time, I was unaware of my actions. Go ahead and acknowledge that you will miss your loved ones, but meanwhile try to remember what the Bible teaches: "Man that is born of a woman is of few days (short life), and full of trouble" (Job 14:1). As for your saved loved ones, they are forever without any more trouble of any sort. And as for those who did not profess to have been born again, they are out of your reach, period. All you can do concerning either case is hold to the sweet memories that you have of the dearly departed. So hold to those precious memories, thanking God for allowing you to have shared a portion of your life with these people.

Death Does Not Disturb the Dead

Part of my pastoral experience has been to get involved with families who inherited the responsibility of putting to rest the body of a departed loved one. I have gotten calls from church members as far as twenty-four hundred miles away requesting assistance. People live as if there shall be no dying. The unfortunate fallout of a practice of that sort is that when the person dies, he or she does not have to bear the burden of putting the body to rest, getting legal matters in order, and dealing with financial matters. That is left to the living.

Interestingly enough, many adult family members live in close quarters (together) for long periods of time without much of a thought about anyone dying. Yet it is a common thing for a member to die unexpectedly. Most of us are not on a precise death schedule of which we are aware. That is to say, most do not know when they are going to depart this world, and death seems to sneak up on them. So it is necessary for us to be concerned about the deaths of our loved ones, especially immediate family members. Chances are good that if you are close to normal, family members' deaths are going to affect you one way or another. But do not allow the enemy of your soul to convince you that you are feeling sorry for the dead. A dead person is not disturbed over his or her personal death.

Unexpected death can often upset the community of even a large family. Part of the problem has to do with their not being prepared for sudden death. Yet we see or hear about sudden deaths almost daily, if only through the news media. But for some reason, almost everyone seems to think, "It is not going to happen to me or to us right now." Therefore, they do not give much thought to death.

The flip side of the above coin, so to speak, is to leave death and all the arrangements up to the person who will do the dying. We develop the attitude that if he or she does not care, why should we? But after that person dies, he or she faces no problems concerning the disposition of the body. He or she has no problem with the unexpected and sudden death or with the legal ramifications resulting from neglected arrangements. Nor does it disturb the deceased that those left behind find it difficult to deal with his or her departure. In short, the deceased is finished with this earthly life and the affairs of life in this world. Those are the things we all need to consider while everyone is still alive and doing well. We need to take time out and prepare for those days that are sure to come as far in advance as possible. It is proper for you to even work to convince those who seem to not be concerned about preparing for their departure in cases where their death will affect you from a logistical standpoint. If they do not want a funeral or burial, suggest that they "will" their remains to the state or some institution that desires them.

The good behind the fact that death does not disturb the dead is that we know our loved ones are not in a state of unrest for any reason. They are not in some dark place anxiously awaiting the sounding of that "first trump." It is a beautiful and comforting thought to be able to release a loved one into the arms of uninterrupted rest. As Jesus said of his friend Lazarus, "Lazarus sleeps" (John 11:11), we too are comforted when we understand that our departed loved ones simply sleep. They are not having dreams of any sort. They are (dead) asleep, meaning no dreams or thoughts or awareness of any kind. Time stops for them. We will discuss the meaning of "sleep" in this context later.

God too is touched by the death of his children. But he is not disturbed; he does not grieve as if his saints have no hope. Death of the saints is precious to him. He understands that our appearing in this world, following the fall of Adam, is for the purpose of our choosing where and how we shall spend eternity. God loves every soul, but he is not bound by his perfect, unconditional love. He loves all his creation. Yet he does not say that the death of the unrighteous is precious in his sight. The unrighteous chose to reject God, which means they failed to choose his eternal salvation. (Let it be understood that this book does not purport to offer comfort concerning those who die without salvation. The truth of matter is that we can never be sure who actually dies without salvation, though some people think they can. But because I can only make assumptions about a person's destiny, I never put such judgment in my own hands.) But the death of the unsaved is not precious in God's sight. At 2 Peter 3:9, the following words are found: "The Lord is not slack concerning his promise, as some men count slackness; but is longsuffering to us-ward, *not willing that any should perish, but that all should come to repentance*" (emphasis added).

No matter how much you recount the idea that your loved one or friend is a saint of God; no matter how many times you declare that he or she is in a better place; no matter how much comfort you find in knowing the person is now better all around, if that person meant anything to you, grief is likely to surface. In fact, it would be a rather sad commentary if no grief were involved. Many take the position of trying to forget the person. Some are even of the persuasion that "not mentioning the person anymore" will cause them to forget him or her faster. The truth of the matter is that you should not want to divest or strip your mind of those precious memories accumulated during your acquaintance with a loved one or friend. Instead, try to make an effort to preserve and cherish those moments. There are so many ways to do it, such as talking about the person, reflecting on the joyous moments you shared, or putting together a scrapbook of pictures and other things pertaining to the person. I sometimes think of a couple of departed friends, and I find myself sometimes thinking about them "out loud," as we put it. I have found myself thinking and smiling as if the person were present at that moment. It is good to keep precious memories alive. There are times I mention to others who knew the same person things that took place with the deceased. We should allow those precious memories to keep on living.

Instead of getting angry with God or with the deceased because of the death, we should try to find a way to acknowledge our appreciation for the time God gave the person in this world. I wish to make this point because too many people get angry either with God or with the deceased. Yes, some get angry with the departed. Neither case is fruitful. Someone might could prove it to be nutty, but not fruitful. They are departed. There is no need to be angry with them, regardless. And it is ridiculously unsound to become angry with God. As a person accuses God of allowing death to befall someone, he or she should also remember that he could allow death to fall suddenly on the angry one. For sure, the devil stands ready to take a person out as soon as possible, especially if he or she is doing good and positive things in the earth. So I am suggesting that we be grateful for the gift of another day to accomplish or experience more of our heart's desires and thank God for having allowed us to know and share in the life of a departed loved one or friend. Again, death does not disturb or grieve the dead. He or she is asleep, just as he or she was before entering into the mother's womb (remember, all were created at the time of the creation of Adam—a truth I will discuss shortly). At Genesis 2:1–3, we find these words: "Thus the heavens and the earth were finished, and all the host of them. And on the seventh day God ended his work which he had made; and he rested on the seventh day from all his work which he had made. And God blessed the seventh day, and sanctified it: because that in it he had rested from all his work which God created and made." In short, God concluded all creation on the sixth day, and on the seventh day—the day he declared, "no more creation of the heavens and the earth, and the hosts therein"—he blessed and sanctified it. I have mentioned Genesis 2:1–3 as a reminder of the truth that every person is asleep until some point during or shortly after conception takes place. The most plain way I can think to put it is that all persons following Adam were first asleep before they entered into the earth, and when they leave here, they are asleep again until the day of resurrection.

Last, concerning the above notion that "every person is asleep until he or she is conceived," I wish to ask a rhetorical question. I wish to ask this question because most people have a mindset that makes it very difficult to see what I am stating. If every person was created at the time of Adam's creation, were they cognizant of their existence prior to conception? In whatever way you choose to answer the question, just remember that the departed return to the Lord. All indications are that each person returns to the very state and position from whence he or she came. What we can be sure of is that our spirits return to God who gave them. And I am sure we were all well prior to conception. No one was restless or impatiently awaiting his day in the earth. And I cannot imagine anyone cognitively awaiting the day of resurrection.

Death Does Not Grieve God

We read at John 11:35, "Jesus wept." There is not a shorter verse in the Bible, yet it speaks volumes. It shows once again the passion of our Lord. He is the perfect God-man. That is to say, he is 100 percent in every aspect of his being. And he perfectly reflects both God and the Son of Man, who in reality are one.

I wish to pause and suggest that Jesus did not weep because of the death of Lazarus as some suppose. Allow me to insert several passages from John 11. Verses 2–4 read, "(It was that Mary which anointed the Lord with ointment, and wiped his feet with her hair, whose brother Lazarus was sick.) Therefore his sisters sent unto him, saying Lord, behold, he whom thou lovest is sick. When Jesus heard that, he said, This sickness is not unto death, but for the glory of God, that the Son of God might be glorified thereby."

When we observe the context of the discussion between Jesus and his disciples concerning the sickness and death of Lazarus, we can see that Jesus did not wish to heal Lazarus of his infirmity. Jesus declared right away that Lazarus's sickness would not lead to (final physical) death. It appears that Jesus was planning on raising him from the dead. Notice he said the sickness was to the glory of God, that the Son of God might be glorified through the matter. Thus, Jesus knew up front that Lazarus was not going to stay in the grave. It would have been awfully strange for him to groan and be troubled in his spirit concerning Lazarus's physical death, seeing as he would rise shortly. Jesus himself said, "Lazarus sleeps." He did not say, "Lazarus is in heaven with the Father, from whence I came. He is there rejoicing in the presence of the Lord." The implication of the Lord's declaration, "This sickness is not unto death, but for the glory of God," is that the death of Lazarus would be brief.

Let us pick this up at verse 32 of John 11 and read through verse 35: "Then when Mary was come where Jesus was, and saw him, she fell down at his feet, saying unto him, Lord, if thou hadst been here, my brother had not died. When Jesus therefore saw her weeping, and the Jews also weeping which came with her, he groaned in the spirit, and was troubled, and said, Where have ye laid him? They said unto him, Lord, come and see." Notice that Jesus observed how the sisters and the crowd were reacting and how they, especially the sisters, were grieved. What he saw brought tears to his eyes. But he did not cry or make a loud noise; he just gently wept. Why? Verse 33 answers the question. When he saw Mary and the others weeping, he was touched by the infirmity of their souls—their grief—and was troubled, and it brought tears to his eyes. He was not grieving on Lazarus's behalf but because of the heaviness and sadness of the living.

The Lord still observes the cries of his people and pities our groans. He still brings comfort to those who will allow him. He is touched by our infirmities. But he will not force his comfort upon us. Mary and Martha did not have to accept the act of raising Lazarus from the dead as comfort. Either one or both could have held on to the thought in their heart, "Jesus could have come immediately and prevented my brother from dying in the first place. He could have saved us from going through this grief." And with such an attitude, they could have remained bitter and rejected the comfort the Lord meant to bring. People do things like that all the time. Instead of being grateful for the fact that God has given eternal life to a loved one, people sometimes let themselves get upset with God for allowing that person to die. We sometimes forget that the person could have been aborted prior to birth or could have died at an earlier age while still in his sin.

Notice now verses 36–38: "Then said the Jews, Behold how he loved him! And some of them said, Could not this man, which opened the eyes of the blind, have caused that even this man should not have died? Jesus therefore again groaning in himself cometh to the grave. It was a cave, and a stone lay upon it" (John 11:36–38). Some of the weepers and onlookers thought it was strange that Jesus seemed to love Lazarus and his family very much. They wondered why he had not used some of that great power he professed to possess to keep Lazarus from dying in the first place. But the reason is clear in verse 4, quoted earlier. Jesus had planned all along to use this event to bring glory to the Son of God. In so doing, verse 45 tells us, "Then many of the Jews which came to Mary, and had seen the things which Jesus did, believed on him."

Though Jesus wept, he knew what the outcome would be. He did not weep for Lazarus. He could comfort himself with the knowledge that Lazarus would soon be returning to his family. Let us understand that things happen soon, and they happen quickly in the sight of God. That is to say, God does not consider time factors in his work. He teaches us that there is a vast difference between his thoughts and ours, his ways and ours. Isaiah 55:8–9 tells us, "For my thoughts are not your thoughts, neither are your ways my ways, saith the Lord. For as the heavens are higher than the earth, so are my ways higher than your ways, and my thoughts than your thoughts." Some things that seem to take a long time to us are quick in the sight of the Lord. (The term "thousand years" literally carries the meaning of "many" or "much time.") Remember that at Revelation 22, the Lord says "I come quickly" three times (verses 7, 12, and 20), but he still has not come with his rewards to give everyone according to their works. That was a long time ago to us. But to Him, his return shall happen quickly.

A point I hope to make is that the Lord knew Lazarus would soon reunite with his beloved family, so he was not grieved about Lazarus's being asleep. Neither would a normal parent or big brother be grieved about a child or little brother having a peaceful and restful sleep. But God knows that those of us who are left behind are very much subject to missing those loved ones and close friends who depart our community and return to the Lord. In some instances, it grieves us terribly, and God knows it. Nevertheless, "Precious in the sight of the Lord is the death of his saints." Although he is not grieved over the death of his saints, as Jesus demonstrated, he can be grieved over the hurt that the living experience. And if we will allow Him, God will reach out and comfort us in our times of pain and sorrow. Never allow your hurt and grief to turn you away from God. When those moments come your way, do all within your power, with the very help of God, to draw closer to him. Especially for the believer in Christ, God will turn those adverse circumstances into glorious blessings in ways you have not yet imagined.

I served twenty years in the military. One common duty roster junior officers fulfilled was called survivor assistant duty. We were assigned the duty of assisting the next of kin of active duty and retired military veterans upon their death. I was exposed to many grieving people over about an eight-year span. Immediately upon retiring from the military, I became an ordained minister, and shortly thereafter I was called to pastoral assignments. My work has included pastoral ministry every since. Through the many years, I have counseled, consoled, offered comfort to, encouraged, and taught what "thus says the Lord" pertaining to the areas that relate to death, dying, and life after death. I have encountered many who appeared to truly love their dear departed kin but actually accepted the fact that the person was gone to be with the Lord and, therefore, considered everything to be all right. There is no question as to whether they missed the departed. Yes, they missed them. But some people learn how to immediately accept the fact death is inevitable. Therefore, they work diligently to release the person into the hands of God. Some are more successful than others in the endeavor. But once we truly understand how wonderful and how precious it is to God when a born-again person departs this life, like God, we too will not grieve for the departed. We might grieve for ourselves or someone else, but not for the departed. (We just observed that Jesus grieved for the survivors, not for Lazarus.)

Many a time, for most of us anyway, we have wished and even on occasions suggested that someone close to us would be free from the hassle and pressure of life for a short while, if not longer. Many of us have been grieved because it was not practical for someone dear to us to just get away from everyday life and rest for a little while. Had it been at all possible, we would have taken on the burden ourselves and allowed them to take a long cruise on a big ocean liner. Or even better, if only we had the power to cause the person to fall asleep and not wake up for thirty days! We would be glad for him or her to have a long and restful sleep.

We do not have it, but God has the authority to conclude, "Well done, thou good and faithful servant: thou hast been faithful over a few things, I will make thee ruler over many things: enter thou into the joy of thy lord," as stated Matthew 25:21 in a parable told by Lord Jesus. Why then would God be grieved if he either calls or allows a servant of his to return to Him? When a person becomes born again, he or she has accomplished God's first and foremost purpose. We learn from Scriptures that God's desire is that all people come to repentance, accepting his gift of salvation. That is because he wants us to spend eternity with him. He, for the most part, leaves saints behind for a season after we are born again because he desires our service in his ministry of reconciliation. But we must never forget that this world is not our home, and God did not send us here to stay.

When God looks upon the death of a saint, he sees a child of his exiting the world of trials and tribulations and crossing the threshold into everlasting peace and joy. And if we are true believers, we should see the same thing. The problem is that we still need to learn how to appreciate the sleep of a saint. I think that it is mostly out of habit that we fail to consider the goodness of a believer's returning to the presence of the Lord. We are so well versed in the dreadfulness of death that we automatically reject the thought of death, especially for someone who was close to us. But I encourage everyone to get acquainted with what the Bible actually says about the life of the dead. (I am confident that if one stays with this book, it shall all become very obvious.)

Chapter Four

What Is Mankind?

Fallen Man Is Frail and Weak

It is a fair question to ask "What is man?" as is asked at Psalm 8:4. We often think in terms of man being frail and weak. In fact, upon the fall of man, he became just that. King David perhaps observed it in light of his own frailty and weakness. The king's questions are rhetorical, but they let us know he is amazed at the fact that the humankind he has come to know appears to be an insignificant creature when looked upon in comparison with so many great things God has created and set in motion. Undoubtedly, when making the comparison, the king recognized the awesome favor he had personally found in the eyes of God and realized that God had been especially good to countless souls in spite of man's adverse conditions.

I am thinking of several commentaries I have read pertaining to Psalm 8, *The Biblical Illustrator* being one of them. The commentaries agree that David was saying that God made man a little lower than God himself. We know that such versions as the King James Version and the New International Version use the phrase "a little lower than the angels." But according to most of the commentaries I have read, the context at Psalm 8 definitely indicates that King David meant "a little lower than God." The Greek term is *elohim*, which sometimes refers to angels or divine messengers from a biblical standpoint as in the case of Hebrews

2:7, where we read: "Thou madest him a little lower than the angels; thou crownedst him with glory and honour, and didst set him over the works of thy hands." The exposition of Psalm 8:5–8 in *The Biblical Illustrator* commentary explains in an understandable manner the fact that man was made a little lower than God.

One thing we need to consider is the state and quality of man prior to the fall of Adam—the perfect state of mankind. Unfortunately only Adam and Eve ever saw a man in the state of a perfect character, save those who beheld the person of Jesus, the Son of Man. Because of our having not seen the true character we were created to be, we tend to get stuck on the revealed imperfection of mankind that we see much of the time. And because of the light in which we see man today, and in David's time as well, we must focus on the Son of Man, who is the only natural man who has spent his entire earthly life in a state of total dominion and power over earth and all the hosts therein.

In light of the above consideration concerning God's creation of perfect humankind, let us further consider that God did not create an irresponsible or imperfect mankind just as he did not create imperfect angels. Lucifer and one-third of the heavenly hosts (angels) fell in sin, but none of them were created in sin. And when God's angels come to mind, we think in terms of perfect beings except for those who fell, which we consider as having been perfect at one time. That should be the light in which we see mankind as well. He became frail and weak only after he fell in sin. Prior to the fall, man did not have to work the earth for his necessities. He was in perfect harmony with God. We think of the act of Jesus's turning water to wine at the wedding in Cana as an awesome feat (John 2:7–9), and some of us talk often about the miracles of Jesus. I am thinking of the five little loaves and two little fish we read about at Matthew 14:17–21.

Jesus is not the only one who exercised dominion over the things of the earth. Consider what we are told at Joshua 10:12–14:

Then spake Joshua to the Lord in the day when the Lord delivered up the Amorites before the children of Israel, and he said in the sight of Israel, Sun, stand thou still upon Gibeon; and thou, Moon, in the valley of Ajalon. And the sun stood still, and the moon stayed, until the people had avenged themselves upon their enemies. Is not this written in the book of Jasher? So the sun stood still in the midst of heaven, and hasted not to go down about a whole day. And there was no day like that before it or after it, that the Lord hearkened unto the voice of a man: for the Lord fought for the Israel.

Yes, it was indeed the power of God working through Joshua. But that is the case concerning all good and perfect things: they all come from God. And throughout eternity, they will continue to come from God. But that is one of many examples of man being given dominion. Just imagine how powerful man was before sin entered the world.

CREATED IN THE IMAGE AND LIKENESS OF GOD

As I study the Holy Bible, observing the relationship between God and man, I am able to understand the awe that was in the mind and heart of King David at Psalm 8. He raised the rhetorical questions: "What is man, that thou art mindful of him: and the son of man, that thou visitest him?" (verse 4). Because David was likely looking at man from his own position, surely he had observed the fact that when Satan and certain angels fell, God made a hell for them. However, when the fall of man occurred, God made a way of escape for him. And through it all, God never withdrew man's dominion over the earth and all the hosts therein. It is sin that has severely impaired man's power and dominion over the earth. Faith has given way to sin, causing doubt and unbelief in many cases. Sin is the very perpetrator that hinders man from exercising dominion. Satan does not have the power to stop you. Had Satan possessed the power, the sun and moon would not have stood still for Joshua for one moment.

Genesis 1:26–27 tells us, "And God said, Let us make man in our image, after our likeness: and let them have dominion over the fish of the sea, and over the fowl of the air, and over the cattle, and over all the earth, and over every creeping thing that creepeth upon the earth. So God created man in his own image, in the image of God created he him; male and female created he them." That is what the Bible has to say. But somewhere along the way, prior to Adam and Eve's first child, sin entered the world and death came by way of sin. Consequently, death passed upon all men (Rom. 5:12).

The Bible does not teach us that the angels or anyone else were created in the image and likeness of God. That is not to suggest that the angels are not in his image, but we are not told they are as far as I can tell. Anyway, I can see that man is not just special but rather most precious in the sight of God. The above passage lets us know that God sees man in a light that is reserved for no other creature or creation of any kind. Some might wish to argue about whether man lost the image and likeness of God, but I am convinced God did not strip man of the image and likeness in which he was created. It is sin, in my opinion, that causes man to not reflect the image and likeness of God continually, and never in the measure of man's creation. Sin did not wound man; it killed him instantly from a spiritual standpoint. It was sudden shock! Man has to be reborn (his spirit reconnected to the spirit of God). And because we exist in a world of sin, we encounter much temptation. We end up yielding to it on more than a few occasions, and that is not healthy for our image.

The question that comes to the minds of many is, "If man is born again, why does he not instantly regain the dominion and power over the earth and all its hosts?" Good question. In conjunction with what I pointed out above, let me illustrate. If you shock a plant to near death by cutting it off from its source of life for any period of time, it will take time for the plant to be revived and to regain the bountiful life it once knew. Something like that has happened to man. Those of us who have become born again do not experience the life man had prior to the fall, although Jesus has come and has made it possible that we be restored not only to life but to life more abundantly (John 10:9–10). But be of good cheer—full restoration shall overtake us as we enter the realm of uninterrupted eternity. I am not of the persuasion that the miracles of Jesus were any greater than those of Joshua from man's standpoint. All power comes from God. But because of Joshua's weakness, he did not have continual dominion over all the earth. Righteous man will regain uninterrupted dominion when all sin is done away with and even death is put under Christ's feet. Do not misunderstand me: we can still experience great peace and joy and exercise dominion. However, we must contend for it. But the day shall soon come when unspeakable peace and joy and dominion shall be our uninterrupted eternal experience. We will once again look and act like our Father which art in heaven.

I mentioned that God did not strip man of his power and dominion when he fell. God did not cast man aside. Instead, he activated a mode of reconciliation. You see, God had already put in place a way of escape from sin and death for man well before man's fall. At Revelation 13:8, we read the following: "And all that dwell upon the earth shall worship him, whose names are not written in the book of life of the *Lamb slain from the foundation of the world*" (emphasis added). Before the world began, the Lamb (Jesus) was slain for the redemption of fallen man. The Calvary event was a manifestation of what God had already done. That is but one of the things that show the mindfulness of God toward man.

The fact that man is made in the image and likeness of God makes a world of difference. John 4:24 tells us, "God is a Spirit: and they that worship him must worship him in spirit and in truth." For sure, God was not talking about the physical body of man when he took counsel with Himself, saying, "Let us make man in our image; after our likeness." Man's body was formed from the dust of the earth. No part of God is earthly. He is 100 percent spirit.

Man possesses a unique composition found in no other creature—the image and likeness of God—and yet lives in a physical body. The Bible says to us at Genesis 2:7, "And the Lord God formed man of the dust of the ground, and breathed into his nostrils the breath of life; and man became a living soul." When we consider what is being said here, we gather that man is an object made by God. We further gather that he was made as a man that did not have a living soul until God breathed into him, through his nostrils, God's own breath (wind or life). We must understand that the breath of God is what caused that lump of clay to come alive. The breath of God, when deposited into the body of man, became what we now know as man's spirit. And when it united with the body, man became a "living" soul. Thus we have body, spirit, and soul.

So, equipped with the above knowledge, it is not difficult for us to see and understand the concept of the triparted man. We should be able to further understand that the term "living soul" suggests the possibility of there being a soul that is not living. Otherwise, such a distinction as "living" would be an unnecessary description of "soul." Personally, it helps me when I see the human soul as if it were a serial number of an object. That is to say, although it is like the other entities of its kind, it can be identified as a precise unit by its serial number. Our souls do not carry serial numbers in reality, but God can distinguish each of us as if we all had separate serial numbers.

If one can relate to the above analogy, it should not be difficult for him to conclude that the word *man* refers to the material or physical (natural) body of a human being, which is his visible and tangible dimension. The natural body is not the eternal part of man, but we are incomplete without a body. From the beginning, man's body required a partaking of the "Tree of Life" in order to maintain animation. However, God made the tree available before he created man. But the spirit of man requires no maintenance or outside substance to remain alive. Though dormant (as I personally call it), the soul begins to function when the body and spirit of man are united. (I am aware of my repeating certain things, but the Bible also repeats certain things. Some things warrant repetition.)

Man's becoming a living soul stems from God's design of him. In other words, God created man's body so that when it comes in contact with the breath of God, it will become a living soul. That is God's special design of man. He could have designed man with no body, but had he done that, it would not have been necessary for man to occupy a physical place such as earth. I know some people think that man does not need a body to function as God intends, but the Bible does not support that thought. It is a stretch of one's imagination that brings one to that conclusion.

I sometimes remind people of the truth that God does not have a baby factory tucked away in the universe. That is, he does not create new souls and spirits as replacements for others in the earth. He completed the creation of souls on the sixth day of creation. I hope that by now we can all understand that every soul and every spirit were created at the same moment, which means that every person is of the very same age, so to speak. What God did was assign each soul (person) an allotted period of time, and he placed people's times at various intervals. God said to the prophet Jeremiah, "Before I formed thee in the belly, I knew thee; and before thou camest forth out of the womb I sanctified thee, and I ordained thee a prophet unto the nations" (Jer. 1:5). The reason a batch of persons are being conceived today is because God is assigning them to earth as he sees fit. Every conception of what some refer to as a fetus is a real person being sent from God by God. And when that person leaves the earth, he returns to God from whence he came. (A side note to the abortionist sympathizers: every time a so-called fetus is destroyed, the earthly life of a person sent from God is denied. And there is no record of God "recycling" fetuses in hopes that the devil allows them to exist long enough to experience a normal birth.)

God designed the human body so it would come alive and function with a special ability that sets it far apart from any other creature, earthly or heavenly. And when he put his life into that otherwise lifeless lump of specially designed clay, according to Moses, "man became a living soul."

The term "living soul" is a key phrase to our discussion. I cannot overemphasize the fact that man is never cognizant of his existence outside of a unity of body, spirit, and soul. Otherwise, man would have to have been cognizant of his existence since the creation of Adam. Surely, every soul that lives at this very moment has been with God from creation until his or her conception. But how much of that period do you reckon you recall?

I pointed out much of the above merely to emphasize that man is directly from God. His true nature is the likeness of God. His true purpose is to commune and fellowship with God. He can scratch and scratch, but the itch shall remain so long as he is not reconnected to the very source that gives true substance to his life. That is to say, only then will he find that his conformity to the image and likeness of God is complete. And seeing that none of us are able to make that achievement on our own, the Lord Jesus Christ has come and has already made it possible through his works, including the shedding of his blood. Thus, it is necessary for us to accept by faith what he has done for us.

MAN IS A FRIEND OF GOD

Jehoshaphat, king of Judah, spoke of God as a friend of Abraham: "Art not thou our God, who didst drive out the inhabitants of this land before thy people Israel, and *gavest it to the seed of Abraham thy friend for ever?*" (2 Chron. 20:7; emphasis added). It is written at James 2:23: "And the scripture was fulfilled which saith, Abraham believed God, and it was imputed unto him for righteousness: and he was called the Friend of God."

Only in a state of righteousness can one be a friend of God. Otherwise, one is his enemy. But in all cases, man proper (righteous) is a friend of God. Jesus Christ also refers to his righteous disciples as friends. He says at John 14:15—16, "Ye are my friends, if ye do whatsoever I command you. Henceforth I call you not servants; for the servant knoweth not what his lord doeth: but I have called you friends; for all things that I have heard of my Father I have made known unto you." God as a friend of man withholds nothing from man that man should know.

Noteworthy is the fact that God does not speak of man as a friend on a casual level or basis. We call people to whom we are not remotely committed friends, but God's sense of friendship comes with total commitment. At John 15:13, Jesus declares, "Greater love hath no man than this, that a man lay down his life for his friends." Most of us know Jesus laid down his life for his friends on the cross at Calvary. Though he died for fallen man, all who would accept his gift of eternal life would once again be his friends. This means you are a friend of God if you are born of the spirit of God.

As our friend, God did not give up on us when we fell. I am mentioning this because I have come across people who were puzzled over the extent to which God seems to be willing to go to reconcile man unto himself. Some have even suggested that perhaps the Bible was exaggerating God's grace or that perhaps man has misinterpreted certain passages that pertain to God's grace, evident in his patience, long–suffering nature, and forgiveness. I am always quick to respond that nothing is being misinterpreted. The Bible describes God's love and friendship very plainly. His unconditional love is bonded in friendship. That is why he is what many of us call the "God of a second chance."

THE ESSENCE OF MANKIND

In making observations on "What is man?" we must not exclude his essence. And we cannot discuss man's essence without reiterating that his core being is a spirit that came from the spirit of God. Is man eternal? Yes. He has a point of origin as man, but not an ending point. His origin came about at the moment he became a living soul, described at Genesis 2:7. God used his own spirit as the core being of man. It happened to every person who shall ever live at any point. We were all created from the breath God breathed into the nostrils of man.

What I wish to point out primarily is that the person we identify as man is not himself three different components, although we often state it as such. But technically the person we call man is a spirit, period. That is why Ecclesiastes 12:7 says the spirit returns to God. However, the Lord brought him into existence and designed him to be housed in a body and to possess a soul. It seems very difficult for most people to grasp the reality of the soul of man being far different from the souls of other earthly creatures. We will get off track anytime we attempt to classify a spirit and soul as being the same in essence. It is true that on occasion the Bible uses the two words interchangeably, but the context of the Scriptures identifies which is being referred to in those instances. One main reason people often fail to grasp certain passages of Scripture pertaining to the portion of eschatology I am discussing is because no distinction is made between the spirit and the soul of man. But for now, instead of discussing the difference between them, let us continue to consider the essence of mankind.

When we take a close look at man from a biblical perspective, we can describe "man proper" as being one made up of the composition of God. It goes back to the very breath, or God's spirit, which he used to create a being like Himself but separate, bearing only the image and traits of his likeness. That is the main reason we are but worms apart from being anchored in God. (Keep in mind that Adam was completely in God prior to his fall.) When we are outside God, we can do nothing—we cannot think rationally, and we cannot enjoy life. In fact, we cannot so much as find peace. Though man's spirit longs to be connected to the spirit of God, his soul seeks to satisfy that longing for things and ideas apart from God in many cases.

In whatever way it is stated, man is designed and created for the chief purpose of being God's companion. He brought us into being so that we can be in constant communion and fellowship with him. Christians often use the terms *worship* and *fellowship*. Do we all understand the meaning of the term *fellowship*? Being in communion and in fellowship means to communicate (talk) together intimately" and to "have a mutual sharing of certain interests, respectively. That kind of intercourse leads to true worship. Observe Genesis 3:8–10: "And they heard the voice of the Lord God walking in the garden in the cool of the day: and Adam and his wife hid themselves from the presence of the Lord God amongst the trees of the garden. And the Lord God called unto Adam, and said unto him, Where art thou? And he said, I heard thy voice in the garden, and I was afraid, because I was naked; and I hid myself." This plainly shows that God had communion and fellowship with man. He did not have to dress himself up in a burning bush. He did not have to get into a wheel in the middle of a wheel. Man knew the very voice of God. And there is no reason to believe that God's voice was necessarily audible as we know natural sounds. I believe God had a custom of coming into the presence of man to hold intimate conversations and to share in certain interests.

It is understandable that when man loses fellowship with God, he loses his true purpose of life. The soul that understands this truth and seeks to be restored to communion and fellowship with God is a person of great wisdom. The person who has been reconnected to the spirit of God is one who experiences peace and joy. Circumstances in life might be far out of tilt, but being reconnected to the spirit of God will produce great substance. We have records of countless people who have experienced being reconnected to God who chose death rather than caving in to demands that they recant their faith in Christ. Many were fed to lions and other beasts, some were burned at stakes, and some bowed to chopping blocks. When man embraces his true essence, he will let nothing separate him from the love of God.

Man Is Custodian of Earth

There is something about earth, its hosts, and the heaven that surrounds it that is unlike any other creation God has brought into existence. At Psalm 8, King David points out things pertaining to the majesty of God. He is fascinated by the splendor of God's favor toward man. In verses 6–9, he declares in amazement, "Thou madest him to have dominion over the works of thy hands; thou hast put all things under his feet: All sheep and oxen, yea, and the beasts of the field; The fowl of the air, and the fish of the sea, and whatsoever passeth through the paths of the seas, O Lord our Lord, how excellent is thy name in all the earth." David takes note of God's giving man charge, with power, over his handiworks concerning planet Earth and all therein. Unlike when we do earthly business, God cannot turn the deeds of anything, not even our own lives, into our hands as if he has nothing else to do with it. All creation is subject to Him, but he has given custody of earth to the children of men (Ps. 115:16).

It amounts to man being God's chief representative in the earth. God does not give man this position as a servant but rather as a friend. In short, God has not made man a keeper of the earth for the purpose of God having an additional dwelling place. Everything in the earth exists for man's provisions and delight. Things are linked together, one attending to another. For instance, the bee attends the fruit tree by pollinating the pistils of its flowers. In turn, the flowers produce fruit. And in the process the bee gets to take away an ingredient necessary in honey making. The bee desires the honey, but bears, of course, think the honey is primarily for them. And when we consider it, man thinks it is primarily for man. Man, however, has profaned things quite seriously in many instances, yet God has not taken the earth from him. But sin has sure enough caused earth to be in a mess.

The bottom line is that God has given man dominion over all the earth. Genesis 1:28 tells us, "And God blessed them, and God said unto them, Be fruitful, and multiply, and replenish the earth, and subdue it: and have dominion over the fish of the sea, and over the fowl of the air, and over every living thing that moveth upon the earth." God created all those things because he is concerned about the comfort and joy of man. We learn at Psalm 115:16, "The heaven, even the heavens, are the Lord's: but the earth hath he given to the children of men." This earth is all about man. That is why God put all things in place prior to bringing forth man. Everything in earth is subject to man. This is man's home, man's world. This is where he was created to live. Earth is the community to which he relates. Most Christians want to go to heaven to be with the Lord, and he wants to come to earth to be with us (Rev. 21:3). One of our main interests needs to be to "take back" what the devil has stolen from us—earth. Praise be to God—he himself shall do just that on the believers' behalf (a new heaven and a new earth).

David observed the fact that God has given the earth to the children of men. The earth was given to innocent man, but as previously stated, he did not withdraw his gift of the earth when man fell. At Genesis 9:1–3, we find the following words: "And God blessed Noah and his sons, and said unto them, Be fruitful, and multiply, and replenish the earth. And the fear of you and the dread of you shall be upon every beast of the earth, and upon every fowl of the air, upon all that moveth upon the earth, and upon all the fishes of the sea; into your hand are they delivered. Every moving thing that liveth shall be meat for you; even as the green herb have I given you all things." This shows plainly that God did not withdraw his gift of earth. Noah's time was years after the fall, but God still charged man to have dominion over the earth. Of course, we have been falling short of God's directions every since the rebellion in the garden. But he still allows us to have dominion.

Because the havoc of the forces of evil is constantly increasing, one can find himself wanting to throw in the towel, so to speak. But as believers in Christ we must hold fast to the charge given us. We do not have to give in to Satan. Sin actually eclipsed man's power to subdue the earth, but it did not blot it out. We do not have to give in to the devil. Yes, in the Garden of Eden, Satan gained the keys from Adam, but at Calvary, Satan lost those keys to Jesus. We still have the charge and the ability to rule over the earth. However, we now must contend for everything good. But once we are clothed in our new spiritual bodies, there will be no more struggle necessary to exercise dominion.

God shall give us a new heaven and a new earth, meaning that even the atmosphere above the earth shall be new. In the meantime, we are to use this temporary earth as a place to worship God in spirit and in truth. All the resources God has put in place for us still belong to us. As born-again believers, we must step up to the plate and act like we are the stewards, the custodians, of the earth that we must occupy until Jesus Christ returns. The forces of evil work against us, but we can yet fulfill our purpose with the help of God. Still, we must by faith call upon the Lord in earnest expectation of accomplishing the things he has purposed for us to accomplish. Remember, although this present earth is no longer our permanent home, it is still our staging ground. We are still to be custodians.

Luke 19:11–13 reads, "And as they heard these things, he added and spake a parable, because he was nigh to Jerusalem, and because they thought that the kingdom of God should immediately appear. He said therefore, "A certain nobleman went into a far country to receive for himself a kingdom, and to return. And he called his ten servants, and delivered them ten pounds, and said unto them, Occupy till I come." This parable represents Jesus's disciples being left behind to occupy until his return. According to *Barnes' Notes* pertaining to this passage, the word *occupy* means to move beyond merely occupation as we normally consider it to mean. It includes making improvements and employing in business for the purpose of causing increase. Thus, Jesus charges us to possess the earth, but not the world system, and to constantly serve to make improvements that are pleasing in the sight of God.

CHAPTER FIVE

God Is Not Insensitive Concerning Death

THE BIBLE IS A BLOODY BOOK

I do not know of a book bloodier than the Bible, especially some of the Old Testament scenes. With reference to the "remission of sin," we learn at Hebrews 9:22 that the remission of sin requires the shedding of blood. It reads, "And almost all things are by the law purged with blood; and without shedding of blood is no remission." In fact, Hebrews 9 is a bloody chapter in its entirety. God loved the world so much that he gave his only begotten Son (Jesus) to die for the sins of everyone in order that whoever would believe on the Lord Jesus could be saved (John 3:16). God does not seem to mind anyone's going to the grave. His love does not keep our bodies from the grave. (The truth of the matter is that his love does not keep us from hell either. Hell will have many souls whom God so loved.)

God has personally ordered countless people put to death. Observe Numbers 32:13: "And the Lord's anger was kindled against Israel, and he made them wander in the wilderness forty years, until all the generation, that had done evil in the sight of the Lord, was consumed." Another example is at 1 Samuel 15:3. It reads, "Now go and smite Amalek, and utterly destroy all that they have, and spare them not; but slay both man and woman, infant and suckling, ox and sheep, camel and ass." Those infants and sucklings especially were not aware of any wrongdoing on their part, but it was ordered that they be put to death.

It was a common event in the Old Testament setting for tens of thousands to perish at the hands of someone God used to teach lessons. He caused all the people above the age of twenty years who left Egypt to die in the wilderness, save Caleb and Joshua, because of their murmuring and disobedient acts. Their actions showed they did not have faith in God (Num. 14:26–31). Those were his people, yet he slew them. We are talking about the same people God used as a pilot, so to speak, to bring about a great nation to call his own.

Back in Egypt, as God was preparing to bring the Israelites out, he killed the firstborn of every person and other creatures that did not belong to the children of Israel. The Israelites were spared because they applied blood to their doorposts, as they had been instructed: "For the Lord will pass through to smite the Egyptians; and when he seeth the blood upon the lintel, and on the two side posts, the Lord will pass over the door, and will not suffer the destroyer to come in unto your houses to smite you" (Exod. 12:23). And do not forget—God drowned Pharaoh's army in the Red Sea to make a point: "Pharaoh's chariots and his host hath he cast into the sea: his chosen captains also are drowned in the Red Sea" (Exod. 15:4).

In addition, let us fast-forward to the New Testament, where we have John the Baptist. The Bible declares that during his days, not a greater man lived. Matthew 11:11 reads, "Verily I say unto you, Among men that are born of women there hath not risen a greater than John the Baptist: notwithstanding he that is least in the kingdom of heaven is greater than he." Still, God allowed King Herod to cut John's head off and display it on a platter. It is common for one to wonder about this person. He was a godly man, and he was a first cousin to Jesus. He preached the uncompromising truth of God. But John was killed without a valid reason from our viewpoint.

And then, there is Stephen, one of God's great evangelists and a church deacon. But God allowed Stephen to be stoned to death for preaching truth. Read Acts 7:54–60:

When they heard these things, they were cut to the heart, and they gnashed on him with their teeth. But he, being full of the Holy Ghost, looked up steadfastly into heaven, and saw the glory of God and Jesus standing on the right hand of God, and said, Behold, I see the heaven opened, and the Son of man standing on the right hand of God. Then they cried out with a loud voice, and stopped their ears, and ran upon him with one accord, and cast him out of the city and stoned him: and the witnesses laid down their clothes at a young man's feet, whose name was Saul. And they stoned Stephen, calling upon God, and saying, Lord Jesus, receive my spirit. And he kneeled down, and cried with a loud voice, Lord, lay not this sin to their charge. And when he had said this, he fell asleep.

It is one thing to suffer or be destroyed because of your own sin or because you are living a life of reproach to the kingdom of God, but we are talking about saints who were upright and without reproach.

We also have the case where King Herod killed a great follower of Jesus, John's (not John the Baptist) brother, whose name was James. We find the account at Acts 12:1–2. "Now about that time Herod the king stretched forth his hands to vex certain of the church. And he killed James the brother of John with the sword." The James spoken of here was one of Zebedee's two sons who Jesus called at Matthew 4:19, saying, "… follow me, and I will make you fishers of men." And when we examine the matter, we are reminded that Jesus predicted at Matthew 20:23, saying, "Ye shall indeed drink of my cup, and be baptized with the baptism that I am baptized with." James was young and in the prime of life, and he had sat at Jesus's feet for more than three years. But God allowed such a wonderful servant as James to fall by the sword of a wicked king.

In today's setting, most of us have witnessed many people becoming angry with God because he did not prevent the death of someone dear to their hearts. Because God views death differently than we do, we see him as being insensitive in many instances. However, if you stop and study the whole scope of God's reasoning and purpose, you will likely conclude that he is not insensitive in the least. It is to the contrary—God is loving and kind and most thoughtful in all his doings. We only need to grasp an understanding as to what is behind God's ways, means, and purposes.

As stated earlier, followers of Christ were burned at stakes or thrown into lion dens often because they refused to recant their faith. And throughout Christian history, to this very day, martyrs have died violent deaths in large numbers. Missionaries devote their lives to kingdom building and sometimes end up slaughtered as a result. In light of this, it is not strange that someone would ask, "God, why do You allow such bad things to happen to good people?" One can find great consolation by reading and studying Revelation 7:13–17.

I, in earlier years, wondered over and over again why would God stand by and allow the devil to have his way with the lives of devout saints. I still watch so many good people die at such early ages. Not long ago, a group of evil men slew the two parents of a group of sixteen children, of which thirteen were adopted. They were a couple who had a heart not only to care for their biological off-spring but to take on thirteen disadvantaged little ones as well. The lives of many right here in America are snuffed out, and we, as believers, know God could have prevented it. But I still say God is far from being insensitive. As news commentator Paul Harvey often said, "Now the rest of the story." We need to understand the rest of the story. And in order to do that, we must unlock the mystery behind God's ways of achieving his purpose.

God Allows the Deaths of Saints for His Glory

Awareness of incidents like I have just mentioned caused me to go on a spiritual quest to acquire a better understanding of why God allows good and innocent young people to die right at what seems to be the beginning or middle of their primes. I read and I studied and I meditated on what I had read and studied. I pondered over those things for years. I was always too full of reverence to accuse God foolishly. I just wanted to know why those seemingly untimely deaths were so often permitted by him as if he were not paying any attention to what the devil was doing. I still have not learned how to put into words what God has revealed to me concerning the matter, but I can assure you that the picture he gives is most satisfying. I have become totally convinced that God is not insensitive concerning life or death. He cares for all without being a respecter of persons. God does not see death as most of us do. Many of us speak as if we have victory over the power of death until it seems near to us or someone dear to us. At that time, death becomes something that is final, and that is the way we treat the idea. For the most part, it finds us far from being ready for that which some seem to view as finality.

Quite a few years ago, I eulogized one of our deceased church members. I shared to the best of my ability my belief that she had lived a full life, although she died at an early adult age, leaving a husband and three very young girls behind. I tried to make two separate points that I felt would console the loved ones and friends, providing they would grasp what I was saying. For those who were somewhat versed in Scripture, my first point was much easier than the second.

I set out to make two main points in the eulogy. First, no one goes to heaven or to hell ahead of the others when he or she dies. In other words, no departed believer is in heaven enjoying the life of promise. Neither is any departed nonbeliever in hell undergoing torture and torment. Second, when a person dies, he or she moves beyond the realm of time into eternity at a speed faster than the twinkling of an eye. There is no gap between time and eternity.

I shall discuss those two points at length, but I also wish to make other points in this chapter in order to help make plain the fact that God is not insensitive concerning the death of his saints.

No One Goes Straight to Heaven or Hell

No one goes to heaven or hell ahead of anyone else when he or she dies. Most people of Christian faith think in terms of departed believers being in a physical heaven where the streets are paved with gold and the saints are going in and coming out and worshiping the Lord. And they think of the unbelievers as being in a lake of fire and brimstone, hot and thirsty. But that is not happening simultaneously to our living on this side of the "day" of resurrection. The departed saints do not have a head start on those who have not yet departed. In other words, no departed believer is in heaven enjoying the life of promise, nor is any departed nonbeliever in hell undergoing torture and torment. (Try to stay with me for a moment.) Why would a hell built for Satan and the fallen angels open prematurely to take in the very people Satan beguiled while leaving him and his hosts behind to roam the world and continually raise havoc?

It is difficult for us to accept the idea that people die and become totally inanimate in every aspect of their being. Being inanimate sounds like one is in some dark holding place, restlessly awaiting animation. But when our senses are not active, we are dead asleep in the truest sense of the word. And being no longer in the realm of time, one cannot register any loss of time or life whatsoever. When I think on this reality, my mind tends to go back to one of the several times I was put to sleep for surgery. Each time when I awakened, my mind picked up right where it had been when I fell asleep. That happens every time the senses of the mind are 100 percent dormant. Therefore, ten thousand years would still be shorter than a moment. I cannot overemphasize the fact that this is the state from whence we all came when we entered into our mother's womb (or the test tube, for some). Some of us might have a difficult time understanding and embracing this reality, but God is not among that group. He knows there is no downtime or waiting period for the departed, but I did not always understand the matter as I do today.

Very often we hear people reflecting on their departed loved ones who were believers, suggesting the person is in heaven, perhaps taking a stroll on streets of gold or perhaps bowing around the throne of God. I have heard suggestions like that even about people who lived a life of sin without any evidence of their ever repenting. Also, I have heard sons and daughters suggest that their dad or mom is walking around heaven doing some of their favorite earthly activities. But let us face the truth. The Bible does not support that idea. With good intentions, we have drawn much stuff from our impression of passages, especially when certain beliefs have been handed down, though they are inaccurate. I think we often fail to investigate certain teachings or doctrines because the sayings are comforting to our hearts just the way they were handed down.

I have heard people refer to Hebrews 12:1 as one of the primary passages upon which they base their belief that saints are in heaven looking down upon those of us on the earth. Any good commentary can help you with that discussion. Hebrews 12:1 says, "Wherefore seeing we also are compassed about with so great a cloud of witnesses, let us lay aside every weight, and the sin which doth so easily beset us, and let us run with patience the race that is set before us." Well, that passage speaks of the saints of the Old Testament and their faith and action as witnesses of faithfulness.

Some of the saints are mentioned by name at Hebrews 11. Verses 4–8 read,

By faith Abel offered unto God a more excellent sacrifice than Cain, by which he obtained witness that he was righteous, God testifying of his gifts: and by it he being dead yet speaketh. By faith Enoch was translated that he should not see death; and was not found, because God had translated him: for before his translation he had this testimony, that he pleased God. But without faith it is impossible to please him: for he that cometh to God must believe that he is and that he is a rewarder of them that diligently seek him. By faith Noah, being warned of God of things not seen as yet, moved with fear, prepared an ark to the saving of his house; by the which he condemned the world, and became heir of the righteousness which is by faith. By faith Abraham, when he was called to go out into a place which he should after receive for an inheritance, obeyed; and he went out, not knowing whither he went.

These are just a few of the old winners who kept the faith. Because there are so many of them, they are referred to as a cloud (a great many) whose acts of faith bear witness that it pays to be faithful unto death. They were the heroes of faith. Some of us today refer to Chapter 11 as the "hall of faith."

It is necessary that I reiterate that Hebrews 12:1 is not suggesting that the departed saints are already in heaven and are watching us run our heavenly race from the bleachers of heaven. The passage is not suggesting to any degree that the saints are somewhere cognizant of their existence. In fact, the word some Bible versions translate as *witnesses* at 12:1 refers to "martyrs" or a "record" of something. It does not correspond to a word such as *spectators*, as many seem to read it. The witness the saints are bearing is this: "Just as God saw them through their journey, he will do the same for you." That is to say, their salvation and favor with God bear witness or attest to the fact that faithfulness pays off. Thus, as God saw them through, he will do the same for you.

It can be painful to entertain the idea that a departed saint does not immediately assume his eternal disposition in heaven from our standpoint of time. This is because our customary viewpoint of heaven paints the picture of a natural setting suspended in a spiritual atmosphere. Somehow our minds seem to condescend God to a figure that we can view as a three-dimensional super object. We tend to see him sitting upon a golden throne made of the purest of precious metals and stones, with Jesus physically seated at his right side. We tend to see the departed saints going in and out of the chamber of God, worshipping him and drinking milk and eating honey. The Bible does give us a figure that resembles such a surrounding, but it is just that—a figure, or allegory. It is given to help us grasp the splendor, the grandeur, the magnificent richness and glorious surrounding of our eternal dwelling place. Our eternal dwelling place consists in the image and likeness of God's all-time dwelling place.

At Revelation 21:2, John saw the holy city, the new Jerusalem, coming down from God out of heaven. John does not mean that a literal, physical city was seen coming down from the third heaven. "Holy city" refers to the home of those who are to spend eternity with the Lord. John's descriptive remarks in verse 2 are intended to paint a vivid picture of the splendor of the new residence of the saints of God. The phrase "coming down from God out of heaven" speaks from a spiritual standpoint of God establishing an eternal, uninhibited paradise that is to engulf the new earth.

The phrase "out of heaven" at Revelation 21:2 refers to heaven with reference to "the sky." It does not mean that God is shipping a new Jerusalem from outer space or from a warehouse somewhere in his place of abode. You see, the heaven in which God abides is everywhere. Scripture does tell us that he is omnipresent. Not only is God in what we on earth view as a foreign heaven, but he is also in the earth ("Repent: for the kingdom of heaven is at hand"—Matt. 4:17). Hopefully, he is in you.

Sometimes our minds get fixed on God residing in a particular locale. But that is not what the writer of Isaiah 66:1 had in mind when he wrote, "Thus saith the Lord, The heaven is my throne, and the earth is my footstool: where is the house that ye build unto me? And where is the place of my rest?" This passage speaks figuratively. It is a figurative picture of the ruling position of God. He rules as King in the sense of how we know natural kings to be. But earth is far too out of place to be used as a figure of his throne. It is but a footstool in comparison.

What I wish to convey is this: heaven is not a physical colony that God has built somewhere beyond outer space as a dwelling place for the saints. Why do most of us view heaven as such a place? I believe it has mostly to do with our lack of grasping the contextual meaning of the term as it applies to each passage of Scripture. A broad definition of the word *heaven* does not necessarily help one to see the biblical interpretation thereof. Stop and think about the definition of the word *heaven*. We have passages of Scripture that tell us God is in heaven—that is true. But we also have passages that tell us God is in those who are born of the spirit of God. Does that mean that when a precious saint dies and goes to be with the Lord, he or she enters into your heart where God lives? I think not. Yet God lives in your heart. But because the Bible tells us that God is in heaven and that when one dies his or her spirit returns to the Lord from whence it came, we think of that person as being in a physical heaven. But we do not think of that person as being located in our hearts in the same sense. However, when we see that same departed person in the light of being a heavenly tripartite, we are going beyond what the Bible actually teaches or even implies. (Perhaps it is time to remind you again of Ecclesiastes 12:7—"The spirit *returns* unto God who gave it").

What John saw and described at Revelation 21:2 is a manifestation in the spirit of the glory and splendor of God that shall surround the saints of God eternally when the presence of God dwells among them in the new earth. But that does not mean that God has to pick up and relocate. He is always everywhere, present all the time. It means that the manifest presence of God will not visit the eternal saints as he did in the Garden of Eden but will continuously dwell among us forever!

What will be good for us to do is stop considering the faithful departed as still existing in a realm of time. They have already moved out of the realm of time and back into the realm of eternity, as they were before they entered their mothers' wombs. How many ways can I emphasize this truth? Therefore, no departed can be somewhere restlessly awaiting the day of the

Lord. They are asleep, at rest, at peace. Time is not passing them by. They are not missing out on anything God has in store for them.

One might ask, "How about all those stories we have heard from people who had what we call out-of-body experiences?" That is another good question. My thought is that it is not easy to believe all those people were lying in the sense that they were attempting to deceive someone. We have had interesting reports from people who have been pronounced clinically dead, and many have been creditable and devout Christians. Some have reported their experiences and have stated that they went directly to heaven. Some reported that they saw indescribable bright lights, and some have declared they saw Jesus. Still others have said they were shown their mansion in heaven. I have heard many different reports concerning out-of-body experiences.

Are all those people making those reports lying to us? Not likely, in my opinion. Is it just their imagination? It is probably not. Saint John, for instance, was all up in heaven, so to speak, and he saw things that had not yet taken place. Paul was caught up as well. He says, "I knew a man in Christ above fourteen years ago, (whether in the body, I cannot tell, or whether out of the body, I cannot tell: God knoweth); such an one caught up to the third heaven" (2 Corinthians 12:2). Keep in mind that it only takes a split second to see anything God wants to show you. It is my humble belief that those who earnestly believe they saw what they reported saw it in the form of a vision. We have no problem believing that biblical characters experienced visions. My guess is that people who feel they had out-of-body experiences actually had something like a vision. I believe those types of visions take place a split moment before or after but not while a person is out of his or her body. I find no basis upon which to accept the idea that they had a vision while they were dead and their souls were dormant. That is my belief. Yet I know that with God all things are possible. But God does not have to violate his own principles to accomplish his purpose.

Perhaps your mind goes to the passage of Scripture above where St. Paul states, "whether in the body, I cannot tell; or whether out of the body, I cannot tell: God knoweth." This is the same case as that of St. John. Paul's spirit had not returned to the Lord from whence it came. That is to say, neither John nor Paul was asleep as in death (dead) when they experienced the visions they share with us. Therefore, their souls were not dormant. Their experiences could be recalled because each person's body, spirit, and soul were still united. Paul is saying he is unable to determine whether or not his physical body actually left earth and rose up to what is referred to as the third heaven as those heavenly things were revealed to him. He said he could not tell—end of story.

I recall sharing in a conversation with several others concerning the movement of the Holy Spirit. Somewhere in the discussion, I recalled an exciting experience I had during a concert of worship one Sunday morning at church. I mentioned that it actually felt like I had been physically lifted up while worshipping in the sanctuary. I remember lifting and waving my hands and arms, and a sense of static electricity was about me. It appeared that I was lifted well above the pews. It was a grand experience. In sharing the occasion, I then made the statement that I could not actually tell whether I was physically lifted up or it just appeared that way to me (I knew my body did not physically rise). My dear wife, however, interjected the reality that it had to be merely a vision. Her reasoning was that had I been physically lifted up, the sanctuary would have immediately become physically empty. I am sure she was right.

We have already pointed out that a person's spirit (the core of one's being) returns to the Lord. We discussed the idea that one is not cognizant of existence except during the period his or her spirit indwells the human body, at which moment man becomes a living soul, whether in a terrestrial or celestial body. For some reason, many great scholars seem to overlook this truth. Nowhere during the course of my study do I recall the Bible referring to man as being a living soul while outside his body.

I mentioned the preceding observation because I wish to discuss several of the many passages of Scripture that are interpreted by most Bible students seemingly to reinforce the idea that all departed saints are already walking around in heaven in their glorified bodies. For the most part, those ideas sound proper, except our interpretation must not leave even one flaw or degree of contradiction. I heard Dr. Frederick K. C. Price say something to the effect of (I am not quoting him), The same key used to conclude an interpretation must unlock every door involved in coming to that conclusion. I strongly agree with the doctor. For instance, many students of certain denominations and renowned scholars hold to the belief that Jesus Christ died on a Friday and rose from the dead the following Sunday morning, and in that time frame he spent three days and three nights in the earth as he said he would do at Matthew 12:40: "For as Jonas was *three days and three nights* in the whale's belly; so shall the Son of man be three days and three nights in the heart of the earth" (emphasis added).

Of course, I am convinced that Jesus did everything he said he would do with no exception.

Some commentaries explain Friday through Sunday morning as being three days and three nights, the commentators accepting such as being within the parameters of the Jewish practice of counting days. That is well and good. I spent twenty years in the US Armed Forces. We too counted any part of a day as a whole day, especially when we were given leaves of absence. But if a person was absent from Friday afternoon or Friday evening through early Sunday morning, we did not declare that he was absent three days *and* three nights. The count would be three days but only two nights. Yet he would be charged with a three-day absence. A couple of commentaries I have read equated the computation of Friday through early Sunday morning as being the same as the count pointed out at the book of Esther. Esther 4:16 reads, "Go gather together all the Jews that are present in Shushan, and fast ye for me, and neither eat nor drink three days, *night or day*: I also and my maidens will fast likewise; and so will I go in unto the king, which is not according to the law: and if I perish, I perish" (emphasis added). The commentators suggest that only two nights were actually involved in the fast of Esther, Mordecai, and company. That sounds great as well. But stop and compare the words pertaining to days and nights in both Matthew and Esther. I italicized the key words that make the difference. Esther simply says, "three days, night or day." She calls for a three-day, nonstop fast. She does not specify that the fast must include three days *and* three nights. But Jesus specifies, and that makes a big difference. In fact, he repeats what he means. He says, "For as Jonas was *three days and three nights* in the belly of a whale…." He took time to specify the time frame. From most people's computations, it appears that Jesus was in the heart of the earth for three days but only two nights.

I have heard quite a few people use Luke 23:43 to justify their conviction that departed saints are in heaven in a state of awareness. There, Jesus is speaking to one of the two men who were crucified on either side of Him, saying, "Verily I say unto thee, to day shalt thou be with me in paradise." Some scholars believe the spirit of what Jesus was saying indicates that the comma is wrongly placed in the King James Version and other versions as well. Of course, the scrolls were not punctuated as we would do today. Such has been added for the modern readers' convenience. But let us go beyond the punctuation and first address John 14:12. It reads, "Verily, verily, I say unto you, he that believeth on me, the works that I do shall he do also; and greater works than these shall he do; because *I go unto my*

Father" (emphasis added). And at John 14:28 we find, "Ye have heard how I said unto you, I go away, and come again unto you. If ye loved me, ye would rejoice, because I said, *I go unto the Father:* for my father is greater than I" (emphasis added). Now, back to John 14:2–3: "In my Father's house are many mansions: if it were not so, I would have told you. I go to prepare a place for you. And if I go and prepare a place for you, I will come again, and receive you unto myself; that where I am, there ye may be also." Addressing the latter passage first, let me remind you that Jesus talks as if it is necessary that he goes to prepare a place before we can be with him in the sense of being aware of our presence with him.

As for John 14:12, Jesus says that he shall go unto his Father (indicating where he shall go when he ascends back to the Father). And at verse 28, he reiterates, "I go unto my Father." The above should lead one to believe that Jesus went back to the Father when he ascended. Other passages state it plainly. Stephen witnessed him at the right hand of the Father, and Scripture tells us he is seated at the right hand of the Father, which refers to a position of authority. Perhaps most of us understand that. But how about what Jesus says at John 20:17? "Jesus saith unto her, Touch me not; *for I am not yet ascended to my Father:* but go to my brethren, and say unto them, I ascend unto my Father, and your Father; and to my God, and your God." This tells me that Jesus himself had not yet gone to the Father, to his God and our God. So why do people conclude that Luke 23:43 is proof of the departed believer going straight to heaven in a state of awareness? They probably come to this conclusion because Jesus indicated that the repentant thief had been accepted into the family of the beloved saints. I believe that most Christians have no problem agreeing that Jesus walked this earth as both the Son of God and the Son of man—we often refer to him as the God-Man. Holding to this thought, remember that moments before Jesus gave up the *ghost* on the cross, he said, "Father, into thy hands I commend my spirit." Thus the spirit of the *man* Jesus also returned to God just as all who die the physical death. As for Lazarus, his spirit was back in his body 4 days after death. Jesus' spirit was back in his body 3 days later.

Some people see Philippians 1:23 as proof that departed saints are cognizant of their presence with the Lord. Here, Paul is speaking, saying, "For I am in a strait betwixt two, having a desire to depart, and to be with Christ; which is far better." Again, we must move into the realm of eternity when we think of those who are departed. Yes, it is better to be present with the Lord. Paul was convinced that he would open his eyes in the presence of the Lord upon his departure from this earth and would be with the Lord forever. But I do not believe Paul was associating his upcoming disposition of eternity with that of time as we know it in this present world. Jesus could not have told the thief who was on the cross, "... tomorrow, you will be with me in paradise." There is no tomorrow in eternity.

My primary aim of discussing Luke 23:43 is to point out that Jesus was not implying that the thief's spirit would bypass returning to God who gave it, as is declared at Ecclesiastes 12:7. Luke 23:43 is not an indicator that believers go directly to heaven and receive their just rewards ahead of saints that are yet to enter into the realm of eternity. From any angle one studies Revelation 20, he must conclude that the dead in Christ do not enter into eternal bliss in the order of their death from a standpoint of time as we know it.

A study of Revelation 20 will show that there shall be a period of judgment for all mankind. (We must keep in mind that the content of Revelation is not presented in chronological sequence.) Yet when we consider the whole of the chapter, it becomes apparent that we all must be judged before there is a presentation and manifestation of our just rewards. And if people have to regroup in order to undergo what is stated between verses 11 and 13, I reckon those who are supposedly in hell will be mighty glad for the break they would get by having to exit hell and go and stand before God. But the Bible does not suggest anything like that will take place. It tells us that all the books will be there, all will be opened, and judgment will flow from all the books, period. I suggest that when you read Revelation, be careful not to misconstrue the word hell with the term the lake of fire and brimstone.

SOULS UNDER THE ALTAR

Oftentimes people read Revelation 6:9–10 and come to the conclusion that there are saints under an altar in heaven restlessly waiting for God to avenge their death. I must acknowledge that it does not take much for one to come to such a conclusion unless he considers the whole of the matter. But in short, the passage does not prove that saints are cognizant of their presence with the Lord. Before we look at Revelation 6:9–10, let us consider Revelation 4:1–2: "After this I looked, and behold, a door was opened in heaven: and the first voice which I heard was as it were a trumpet talking with me; which said, Come up hither, and I will shew thee things which *must be hereafter.* And immediately *I was in the spirit:* and, behold, a throne was set in heaven, and one sat on the throne" (emphasis added).

This helps us to understand that John saw what was in the future from our earthly standpoint rather than in the present time. That is to say, when we view it from a perspective of time, the future, not the present, was being revealed to him. The Lamb of God was slain from the foundation of the world (Rev. 13:8). Christ's crucifixion, however, was not manifest until about two-thousand years ago. What is being said in Revelation 13:8 is that in eternity (past), the Lamb is slain from the moment that God determines it should be done. But in the realm of time, the event took place much later.

Now back to Revelation 6:9–10. The passage reads, "And when he had opened the fifth seal, I saw under the altar the souls of them that were slain for the word of God, and for the testimony which they held: And they cried with a loud voice, saying, How long, O Lord, holy and true, dost thou not judge and avenge our blood on them that dwell on the earth?" Here John is observing the fifth seal being opened. This seal relates to the invisible. It might help if you are reminded that there is no need for an altar for sacrifice in heaven. What John is shown is a figure and a symbol. Martyrs are they who sacrificed their lives for the cause of Christ, and standard practice was to pour the blood of that which was sacrificed at the base of the altar. (Perhaps you would like to observe Leviticus, Chapters 4, 5, and 9 for a more detailed picture.)

I will get back to Revelation 6:9–10 in a moment. Meanwhile, let us read Revelation 5:6. "And I beheld, and, lo, in the midst of the throne and of the four beasts, and in the midst of the elders, stood a Lamb as it had been slain, having seven horns and seven eyes, which are the seven Spirits of God sent forth into all the earth." This is an example of the figures and symbols John saw while he was in the spirit. Beginning at Revelation 2, there are lots of symbols and figures, to include Revelation 6:9–10. In relation to Old Testament observance, martyrs were looked upon as sacrifices. The souls underneath the altar are symbolic of those who had given their lives for the cause of the kingdom of God.

The term *souls* in the context of the above passage refers to individuals, and the term *spirits* could have been used and would point to the very same articles. Anyway, the cry of the souls is not an audible articulation of the actual voices of a group of martyrs.

The figure shown to John is on the order of what is stated at Genesis 4:10 by the Lord when speaking to Cain, who slew his brother Abel. The passage reads, "And he said, What hast thou done? The *voice* of thy brother's *blood* crieth unto me from the ground" (emphasis added). Of course, God could hear the cry of the voice of Abel's blood, but neither Abel himself nor the voice of his blood was the cause of his blood's articulation. Nothing in the passage suggests that Abel or his blood was cognizant of the cry. The same is true concerning the souls under the altar of which John speaks. Luke 19:40 is another example of such a figure: "… I tell you that, if these should hold their peace, the stones would immediately cry out." God is able to hear whatever he wishes, but I do not think the stones would have been aware of their cries.

According to *Jamieson, Fausset and Brown's Commentary on the Whole Bible*, as well as others, the altar discussed in Revelation 6:9–10 is in the earth rather than in heaven. The commentary explains quite well the fact that the altar John mentions is symbolic of the altar on earth. I have read several commentaries that take time to explain the symbol quite well. However, some commentaries lean to the notion of the departed saints' being fully awake and fully cognizant of their heavenly surroundings. Of course, as I have discussed all along, this is true only in the sense that when one departs, in the twinkling of an eye, without missing a beat, he is raised from the dead and caught up to meet the Lord in the clouds or in the air, or in the heavens—however one prefers to state it.

From Time to Eternity

We pointed out earlier that when a person dies, he moves beyond the realm of time. And with this understanding, I am able to recognize the fact that from the very first death—let's say it was Abel, Adam's first son—to the very last person who will die, the inclusive period they remain dead is too short to measure, the same as "no time," period. This idea suggests that Abel has not been dead any longer than your great-great-great-grandparents. In fact, in the sense that I speak, Abel has not been dead any longer than the last person who will die today or any time in the future. The point I wish to make is that the period between the death of a person and the resurrection of the same cannot be measured in time. From where (in eternity) would you come across time? The reverse of that reality is that from the creation of Adam, of which everyone was included, to your inception into your mother's womb, you spent no time, although you were created when Adam was created. This reality can be illustrated with a mustard seed that has been around, well preserved, for thousands of years. The seed finally gets put into good soil and germinates and grows into a beautiful plant. The seed was actually the plant all along, but the plant did not manifest until it came forth through germination and growth. I am saying that the plant in reality is as old as the seed. And in terms of man, unlike the mustard seed, he reverts back to that dormant soul he was before he entered the good soil of his mother's womb.

THE MEANING OF ETERNITY

Let us move to a discussion concerning eternity. A quote from the Lord is provided at Isaiah 43:13: "Yea, before the day was I am he." And from 2 Peter 3:8, we read, "One day is with the Lord as a thousand years, and a thousand years as one day." Peter lets us know that God does not see time in the same light as we who are creatures that can think and operate only in time. Before anything ever began, God always was and is. He says, "I am," an example of eternity. Peter wants us to know that it makes no difference to God if we consider one day or a thousand years—it is all the same with him. Think about it. It all equals the same in eternity.

My discussion of time versus eternity is brought to the surface for a twofold purpose. First of all, how can we measure the distance in outer space unless we find two reference points? We must have at least two poles or points in order to determine time or distance. Without two points, we must declare it to be infinity. That is actually what eternity means. It is not fixed with an end. Now, in one sense, a person can hold to the idea that eternity has a beginning except in the case of God. But one could argue that eternity proceeds from God, and once we step into eternity we shall have no end. That appears to be a moot point, though someone may choose to debate it.

The other discussion of time versus eternity has to do with our being reminded that God operates from a standpoint of eternity even when he reaches into time. That is why Jesus said slightly more than two-thousand years ago, "And, behold, I come quickly ..." but still has not come. In that same light, God allows his beloved children to depart the earth and does not consider this departure to be a bad experience on their part. God knows his children shall spend no restless time someplace waiting to be raised from the dead.

We die and enter into eternity. We do not have to deal with any Big Ben clock, period. Zulu time is no more. No measurement of time is considered. And because one is not cognizant of his or her existence prior to resurrection, not one moment is realized until we all are either resurrected or changed and come before the Lord. We all enter the presence of the Lord in a state of awareness at the very same point.

Now, because there will be no more dying, nor will there be any further status change for the deceased, eternity is in force immediately upon death rather than being delayed until the point of resurrection. Again, this is because the spirit of everyone who dies returns to the Lord. But no sooner than one's spirit, body, and soul unite does one become cognizant on the spot. I had an experience in an operating room that helps to illustrate the point I am trying to make.

During my stint in the military, I underwent back surgery. My assigned nurse was a young female lieutenant who had recently entered with a direct commission. She was an experienced nurse but an inexperienced soldier. I delighted in advising her concerning military affairs whenever she came around, and she spent quite a bit of time with me. On the day of my surgery, the lieutenant personally prepared me for the operating room and injected me with a shot of what I referred to as "happy juice." The shot is given to make patients relax just before being taken to the operating room. The happy juice increased my urge to talk and joke around, and I did not hold back. I recall talking nonstop all the way to the operating room. And rather than counting, I talked myself to sleep.

Several hours later, the surgery was finished and I awoke, or at least became aware of my surroundings there in a recovery room. My lieutenant was the first person I saw. Believe it or not, I picked up right where I left off. I felt no pain and did not know the surgery had taken place. I recall inquiring as to when were they going to perform the surgery. Time never stopped for the lieutenant and the rest of the surgical team, but time stood still for me during those hours I was under the gas. Of course, activities all around me and literally in me took place while I slept, but I knew nothing of it. The only reason I say time stood still in this instance is because I reentered it right where I had left off—on this side of eternity.

Had I not reentered time (awakened), I would have moved into eternity. My point is that I picked up right where I had left off. In terms of my awareness, I was in the operating room a very short period of time, and within almost no time I ended up in the recovery room. Keep in mind that the people in the operating room who were not put to sleep moved right through what was downtime to me. That parallels with the living and the dead. What happened to me is that I lost consciousness or awareness of my existence, though I did not cease to exist. Again, time never stopped because I did not enter into eternity. But because I was not personally aware of my existence to any degree, it was as if I were suspended outside of time.

Allow me to share one more illustration. I do not recall his name, but some years ago a young man was involved in an automobile accident in which he received an acute blow to the forehead, and he went into a coma for nineteen years. He was the father of a young baby when the accident happened. The report is that when he awakened, his mind was completely registered on the last things he remembered prior to the wreck. The man could not accept the person who had become a twenty-year-old young lady as the daughter he knew as a baby nineteen years earlier. The last I heard, they had not been able to convince the man that the young lady presented to him was in fact the same person he had known as his little baby. To the people around him whose lives had not been disrupted in a manner like this, those nineteen years were spent. But to that man, those nineteen years had never occurred.

How difficult is it to understand that when a person moves from the realm of time he enters into a state of eternity? Therefore, being in a state of eternity and unaware of his existence, one is asleep, as Jesus put it referring to Lazarus at John 11:11. Had Lazarus been in heaven, in the bosom of Abraham, or in Paradise in a state of awareness, he would not have been described as being asleep. He could not be asleep and awake at the same time.

When we leave our physical bodies, we enter a state of rest as we return to God. God does not count it as our being robbed of life any more than you would count your child as being robbed of life when he lies down to take a nap. Perhaps at times there would be other playmates around the house and your child would rather be playing with them instead of sleeping. That would cause the child to dread going to sleep. But as his parent, you know that when he awakens, there will be plenty of time for more fun, and perhaps the trip you have planned for him to Disney World will be even greater fun than he is already experiencing. Let me state that the child, once asleep, would not have any problem with the rest he would be getting.

Well, in a much greater way, God does not count it as robbery when a saint is called to rest. Remember, "Precious in the sight of the Lord is the death of his saints," says Psalm 116:15. It is in fact God's delight to say to a saint, "Well done, thou good and faithful servant" and then invite him or her to come up higher and rest.

Understanding Eternity Will Perhaps Remove Fear of Death

When I grasped the reality of moving from time to eternity, I was relieved of the dread of death I had wrestled with most of my life. I began to understand how a good God could allow good people to die young, a thing we commonly call an untimely death. The fact came to me that God knows quite well there is no loss of life for any saint.

You see, to the living it looks like former president George Washington has been dead a long time. But in reality, the period of time between the first president of the United States of America taking office and that of the current one lies within the minds of those who are alive, not the deceased. We measure time by the rotation of the earth around the sun. If we had no means of determining time, it would not be difficult to accept the idea that President Washington has not been dead very long. As stated before, the measuring of either distance or time requires two points. John records at Revelation 21:20–25, "And the city had no need of the sun, neither of the moon, to shine in it: for the glory of God did lighten it, and the Lamb is the light thereof. And the nations of them which are saved shall walk in the light of it: and the kings of the earth do bring their glory and honour into it. And the gates of it shall not be shut at all by day: for there shall be no night there." With the above in mind, how can one measure time in eternity? What would be the significance of time?

The deceased are not in some place or a state of being restless because they want to rise again. They are beautifully asleep, a sleep that is perhaps very similar to the way yours would be if you were put to sleep in an operating room and kept alive until the day of the rapture, at which time you would become changed and caught up in the clouds to be with the Lord. You would have gone to sleep perhaps while you were trying to count to ten, and before you could say the next number, you would find yourself in the presence of the Lord.

I mentioned earlier the back surgery I underwent many years ago. I had known for several days that I would be having surgery, and I knew they would put me to sleep. But that did not disturb me in the least. I suspected that during the time I would be asleep, I would not be aware of anything taking place. In fact, I did not *want* to be aware of anything. My point is that I had no fear or dread of being put to sleep. Why not? Because I believed I would wake up, my back would soon heal, and my back problem would soon be gone. I had no fear of the doctors' failing me, so I did not hesitate to put my life in their hands, so to speak. In similar manner—but to a much, much greater measure—I do not hesitate to put my life in God's hands. It is because I am convinced that when I die, I will rise again. I am convinced there will be no downtime between my natural death and my resurrection. Therefore, I have nothing to fear. Likewise, if you are born of the spirit of God, there is nothing you should fear either. Dying will be no different from being put to sleep in an operating room and remaining asleep until you are awakened. I can tell you, you would wake up right where you left off as far as you would be concerned. And your concern is what matters.

Some people read about how Jesus, in the garden of Gethsemane (Matthew 26:39), agonized over the bitter cup of which he was about to partake. To many, that gives them just cause to fear and dread death. Jesus was about to go through something we could never come close to experiencing. First of all, consider what is pointed out at Hebrews 13:5: "… for he hath said, I will never leave thee, nor forsake thee." That means that when a saint suffers for the sake of the kingdom, he does not suffer alone. God is by his side. But that did not apply to Jesus. He was to be separated from the Father from the sixth to the ninth hour while he bore the sins of the world. That was the part of the cup Jesus dreaded. We have no idea what it meant to him to be totally separated from the eternal Father—with whom he had been in union throughout eternity—as he would be bearing the sins of the world. A better way to put it is that he would be separated from himself. That makes the difference. We do not have to worry about bearing the sins of the world and becoming separated from our own beings, but Jesus knew beforehand that it was going to happen to him.

I wish to make a point concerning the difference between dread and fear. Most of us have not come to a place of being free of dread, especially when it comes to dying. Your dread may well be one of having to die a physical death. The bottom line is that believers often dread death for various reasons. It could be unfinished works you wish to accomplish that cause dread, or it could have to do with the fact that you wish to see your child or grandchild reach a particular milestone in his or her life. That is all well. But do not allow the adversary to influence you to interpret dread as fear. If you are confident that you will rise again, you have no reason to fear death. Fear is a trick of the enemy of your soul.

Death is no longer our enemy if we are born of the spirit of God. Remember the poem "Death Meets His Maker" mentioned earlier. In it, Death becomes a humble servant to the saint, saying something to the effect of "I just push open the gate and help the saints get home" (that is not a direct quote). The truth of the matter is that death is merely a threshold that leads to everlasting life. I pray that saints of God do not allow Satan to intimidate them with the thought of death.

GOD ORDAINED DEATH AS PART OF THE PROCESS OF HIS PURPOSE

Death plays a major role in the process God has ordained to accomplish his purpose. We stated much earlier that death involves separation. When man sinned, he became separated from God. And because of man's sin, God sanctioned man to become separated from his sin-contaminated body. God is in the process of doing away with everything that sin has stained. He is not willing to dwell with any appearance of sin, yet he desires to spend eternity with mankind. Thus, God uses the process of death to achieve his purpose of separating redeemed man from his old, sin-contaminated body and bringing him into his new, celestial body. The same process is used to remove all mankind from our earthly house. But it does not grieve God to allow his saints to come home. He knows and understands that they will be weary no more. Remember what Revelation 21:4 tells us: "And God shall wipe away all tears from their eyes; and there shall be no more death, neither sorrow, nor crying, neither shall there be any more pain; for the former things are passed away." Gee! Had God chosen to allow man to spend an eternity in a sinful body, which would have meant man could never be in a position to have the uninterrupted eternal communion and fellowship that God desires with us, then one might have a reason to think that God is insensitive about the fate of man.

In spite of the above discussion, it is not hard to draw the conclusion that God is insensitive about death if we do not move beneath the surface of the matter. On the surface, the only time someone's leaving the earth seems to concern him is when he has further purpose for the earthly life of that person. That is, when it serves God's purpose to leave someone here, he does it. I personally am a living example of one getting a second chance on life. God has intervened several times on my behalf. He has done it for many of us, whether or not we have paid much attention to it. Satan is constantly trying to take you out. But there are cases in which God has a special purpose for a particular person, and the devil and all his hosts shall not be able to take the person out until God dismisses him.

I often think of how many times biblical characters such as the apostle Paul had near-death experiences and God delivered them. But in the end, Paul, for instance, when he had finished his course, was beheaded. It did not happen until God was satisfied that Paul had finished his earthly assignment.

Earlier, we mentioned Stephen, who was stoned to death. He was a young man in comparison to the apostle Paul at his death. Stephen's body probably had many good miles left in it, but God did not prevent his death. God does not see us in a light of having a loss of life simply because we do not spend as much time on earth as someone else might spend.

The fair and equal-opportunity coach of a children's basketball team who calls a player to the bench and sends in a replacement does not do it because he either likes or dislikes his players. He does it as part of his strategy to play and win the game. God too has a strategy. He has purpose for each of his players of the kingdom of God. The major difference between God and some fair basketball coach is that God is perfect in all his ways. All that he does is exactly the way it should be done. But like that parent of the little fellow that the coach pulled off the court, sometimes we do not understand why God would allow our loved ones to be pulled off the court of life. But God knows.

Keeping with the analogy of the coach and the basketball players, the one pulled off the court does not get dismissed from the team. Whatever the team accomplishes, he remains a part of it. The same is true with God's team of winners. We all get called to the sideline at some point. Some members get to play longer, but we all must finish our course. Unlike the parent who thinks more highly of his or her child than of the team at large, the coach is not grieved over the fact that he had to pull one out and put another in. He knows that when the championship is won, the whole team wins. And even more, God is concerned about the championship. Every believer on his team shall be a winner.

Chapter Six

Consolation for the Bereaved—The Message in a Nutshell

The Last Breath

We cannot follow our loved ones beyond their last earthly breath. We, for the most part, tend to see them as having gone off and left us behind. In one sense, that is what happens. But in another sense, believers who die in Jesus Christ will remain 100 percent asleep until all born-again believers are caught up together to meet the Lord in the clouds (1 Thess. 4:17). Thus, they will not miss a step in life. No matter how long ago someone's death may appear to have been to the living, the deceased senses no time loss whatever.

Until we comprehend the zero time frame between the end of the last earthly breath that one takes and the resurrection of that same person, we will probably continue to see the deceased as being stuck somewhere in a holding place of which they are aware. Some see them as being in heaven, going to and fro among God and the heavenly hosts. But we should let go of that myth. The dead in Christ will not come down from heaven when Jesus returns for the saints. They will rise, not descend (1 Thess. 4:16). In fact, they will first rise and, together with the living, then be caught up in the clouds to meet the Lord in the air. Thus, both the quick and the dead shall see the Lord face to face at the same moment.

CONSOLATION IN THE RESURRECTION ASSURANCE

The words the apostle Paul gives at 1 Thessalonians 4:18 are words of consolation to the believer as it pertains to himself and as it pertains to his loved ones, whom he believes are saints of God. In fact, Paul's final words in Chapter 4 exhort us to comfort and encourage each other with the information and teaching he shares with us. God does not want us to fall apart because we lose a loved one or friend. He gives us the necessary information to find consolation.

We who believe in the resurrection of Jesus Christ from the dead are reminded that as God raised Him, so shall he raise those who die having faith in Christ. The assurance of the resurrection of the dead in Christ follows from the truth of the resurrection of Jesus himself. At 1 Corinthians 15:14, Paul declares, "And if Christ is not risen, then is our preaching vain, and your faith is also vain." Thus, the foundation of our hope is established not only upon the cross but upon our Lord's resurrection from the dead as well. And the apostles and many others bore witness that Jesus Christ arose from the dead. The apostles were willing to give their lives because they believed God would also raise them from the dead in like manner. And, by faith, that is the hope of every believer. Furthermore, I have read in several sources that secular history bears record of the fact that Jesus returned from the dead.

STRIVE TO COMMIT THE DECEASED TO CHRIST

You must strive, though it might be difficult, to truly commit the deceased back into the hand of God from whence everyone came. From our biblical account, God created Adam and all mankind thousands of years ago. And as we consider it, all mankind was created at the same moment, but only Adam was actually walking about in the earthly realm for a period of time. And then came Eve. This means thousands of years on earth took place before some people were manifested, and some still have not yet come. But think about it. Whether it was one thousand years later or six thousand years later, every person who comes into the earthly realm comes without having been somewhere else, anxiously waiting on his or her appointed time. He or she was with God (Ecc. 12:7) from creation until entering into the mother's womb. Do not forget that God has no baby factory in the heavenly realm. He took care of the creation of all mankind in Adam. And the above-referenced passage of Scripture declares that every person returns to God. And that is a good clue. One cannot return to a place he has never been at some prior point.

It is much easier to suggest it than it is to actually commit a loved one into the hand of God without grieving. It requires far more than a notion to suddenly let go. Yet the sooner you can let go, the better it is for you. Knowing that somewhere along the line you will likely face bereavement, it is wise to consider the fact of the matter beforehand to the best of your ability. However, that does not mean you will not grieve. But while you grieve, you need to be able to stand firmly in the truth of the knowledge that the deceased is in no way uncomfortable, restless, or anxious for anything.

Like it or not, everyone leaves here. The Bible tells us that a man called Enoch and one called Elijah departed earth without seeing death. But I am convinced that they did not go to heaven in their earthly bodies because, without exception, flesh and blood cannot inherit the kingdom of God. And we get no hint that either one of them has received his glorified body and is in heaven walking around and conversing with the Lord. I must conclude that they too returned to the Lord from whence they came. Yet they will not miss a step. And as for what happened to the earthly house they lived in, I cannot explain. But Jesus was also seen as he was being received into the cloud while still in his house. Yet we would not likely believe he went home in that earthly tabernacle and is somewhere restricted to a body, and I sure enough cannot perceive that he has parked his body in a heavenly warehouse or storage closet. The idea of Jesus's being seated at the right hand of the Father causes some to imagine that he is physically sitting beside the Father in a great big chair. Do not forget that God is spirit and Christ is also spirit, seeing that he is God and we have but one God. God is present everywhere. Trust me—Jesus is not stationary in some precise location, tied down to a physical body and having to send himself out in the manner of radio frequencies traveling through the air.

It is important for the bereaved to strive to take on the attitude that King David displayed at 2 Samuel 12:15–23. All the while his son was sick, he prayed and fasted, and he would lie all night on the ground. This went on for seven days; the king grieved and moaned the whole period, neither eating nor talking. But no sooner than he learned his child was dead did he arise from the ground and wash and groom himself. He then went into the house of the Lord and worshipped God, after which he went home and ate.

The minds of the king's servants were boggled over his behavior. They were puzzled over the fact that while his son was alive, though sick, the king would not eat or talk or come into his house. But as soon as the child died, the father arose and began to act as if nothing was wrong. That is a picture of beauty once you take into account the whole truth concerning the life of the dead. King David realized that he could not hold to his child once he was dead.

David simply committed his son to the Lord. He had fasted and interceded while his son was alive. Chances are, he prayed to God that his son might live. But when he realized that his son was deceased, he understood there was nothing further he could do on behalf of the child. Therefore, he committed his son's spirit back to the Lord from whence it came.

Does David's behavior following the death of his son suggest that he immediately got over the matter? I believe not. I believe the father's heart was still sad. He still sensed the loss he had suffered, but he perhaps reasoned that there was nothing left he could do. The matter was strictly out of his hands. Thus, David chose to be strong and perhaps encourage himself in the Lord and in the hope of the resurrection. And that is what I pray we will try to do today.

Equal Time for All

Our creator is totally impartial in all his ways. The problem is that we fail to understand all his ways of dealing with us. Seeing that we live one moment at a time and are never able to reach back and reoccupy any past moment, we remain in the moment as we move from what we consider one moment to the next. This means that time is an individual matter. No one lives another person's moment. I am thinking of the fact that one called Methuselah lived about 969 years, yet he actually lived no longer than a newborn baby who dies shortly after birth. The baby lives moment by moment, and all the way through those nine-hundred-plus years, Methuselah only lived moment by moment. What causes the matter to be the way it is has to do with the fact that all the bygone moments are merely history of what has come and gone. If you live two days, yesterday is history and is reserved only in your memory. If you live two thousand years, yesterday is still history and is reserved only in your memory.

God understands this. Because he knows and understands very well his own design for man, God does not consider it robbery of mankind when he allows him to cease living in the realm of time. After all, a person who is born today has been with God since the creation of Adam. Thus, if

God were to measure and decide based on time, perhaps he would consider that if one has spent more time with him without his body and spirit being united, one is not short-changed, so to speak, by returning to him until all his children are united in their glorified bodies. I hope you are getting this. I am saying that if God was not insensitive when he allowed you to remain with him from the life of Adam until you were conceived, on what grounds could you think him to be insensitive for allowing you to return to the very state from whence you came?

In light of the above conclusion, God is not showing himself to be a respecter of persons when he allows some to live on earth for only a short period of time while others live much longer. Never forget, the death of a saint is precious in his sight (Ps. 116:15).

TODAY'S EARTH IS MERELY A STAGING GROUND FOR MANKIND

Contrary to popular assumption, we do not exist for our own pleasure and glory. It is true that most of us have come to really like this place regardless of its sinful condition. But the condition of the earth is not like it was when God first created man. He first put man here as a being that was created in his own image and likeness for the purpose of communion and fellowship with God. Even at that time, he already knew man would fall from the state of innocence in which he was created. And foreseeing this fall, we learn that the Lamb of God was slain before the foundation of the world (1 Pet. 1:20). This means that God had already planned a way of escape for those who would choose to be with him throughout eternity. Why did God make this plan? He did it because it would allow man to elect to come back to God or go to hell.

With the knowledge God had of man's future conduct and behavior, he set everything in motion that would serve his divine purpose. He dressed the Garden of Eden for man, putting a forbidden tree in the midst thereof (Gen. 2:17). This gave man the opportunity to choose obedience or disobedience, good or evil.

God knew all along what decision man would make in every step of life. This means he knew man would be tempted by Satan and would yield to temptation. But all this played right into God's hand. The once high-ranking Satan, who had been known in heaven as Lucifer, was bringing God's purpose to fruition.

And when the fall took place, it became the right and responsibility of man to choose whether or not he wants to spend eternity with God. Before temptation was introduced, man was simply innocent. He had no part in choosing his fate. But we must understand that God desires complete glory. This kind of glory comes only via man's voluntarily choosing to be with the Lord. And in a nutshell, that is why we have to undergo so many trials and tribulations today. We have to strive or contend for the faith. We have to uphold certain laws and principles of God if we want to spend eternity with him. And so God gives us the opportunity to choose where we desire to spend eternity. The rest of the time we get on earth has to do with giving us opportunity to help him advance his kingdom. Thus, when a saint of God dies, it is not a loss to the departed. If anything, it has to be considered a loss to God in that the servant was, or should have been, in the process of helping God to advance his kingdom. But in too many cases, it is no loss to God in the least. Like the just coach mentioned in Chapter 5, God has plenty of players on the sideline who will enter the mother's womb upon command, so to speak.

Before I move on, I wish to point out the amazing thought that the same Lucifer was the one who brought glory to God in heaven. You see, all the heavenly hosts were in the same position as Adam and Eve. They had not been put in a position to elect to be with God. When the angels knew anything they were in the presence of God as in the case of Adam and Eve. They were totally innocent. But when Lucifer rebelled against God and tempted the heavenly hosts, two-thirds of them chose to remain with the Lord God. That was an election process. Thus, that two-thirds of angels are his by their own choice, and that brings glory to God. He now allows man to choose or reject him. That is why he releases us to come here in spite of our fall through Adam. We are getting a second chance, and God is getting souls that delight in being with him. But because we all fell in sin through the acts of Adam, we have to prove ourselves through the process of trials and tribulations. We have to take up our cross and follow Jesus daily (Mark 8:34). God is looking for souls who have been tried and found true. Those acts I am pointing out are not the acts that save us. We are saved by grace through faith. But once we become saved, we are challenged through trials and tribulations. And the spirit of God residing within us compels us to hold to God's unchanging hand regardless of the challenges we face.

I know the suffering we undergo hurts a lot of times. God knows it better than I do, yet he not only allows us to go through tribulations, but he has ordained that we suffer them. However, I have to agree with the apostle Paul, who says, "For I reckon that the sufferings of this present time are not worthy to be compared with the glory which shall be revealed in us" (Rom. 8:18). And I say to you that God allows us to suffer only because he wants us to really prefer him over our short earthly lives. He basks in the glory wrought through our choosing to suffer for his name sake. But the reward God has in store for those of us who endure to the end shall be much greater than the suffering. And the reward is eternal, whereas the suffering lasts for only a little while.

A Call to Discipleship

Since reading this book, I trust you have received some food for thought and have lost fear of death, if you had any in the first place. I pray that in the process, you have come to grips with whether or not you are prepared to spend eternity with God upon departing this present life. Thus, if you have not already accepted Jesus Christ as your savior and lord, let today become the defining moment of your life. Accept his gift of eternal life.

Do not try to come to Jesus with the idea or attitude of accepting him for the purpose of staying out of hell. God wants you to come to him out of a desire for him; he wants to be your choice, first and foremost. He wishes you to desire to be with him as he desires to be with you. Therefore, I encourage you to ask Jesus, in your own words, to accept you into his eternal kingdom and earnestly declare to him that you will make him Lord of your life and gladly accept his gift of salvation, which comes as a result of your wanting to be with him. Too many people try to accept Jesus as a mere means of escaping hell. That will not work. That is why you find so many people who claim to be Christians but are living like the devil. They do not want the heart of Jesus. They wish only for his hand. That is to say, they wish for only the benefits he offers.

It is not necessary to ask the Lord to forgive you of your sins past; he has done that already. Instead, give thanks to him for having done so. Do not worry about praying what has been termed The Sinner's Prayer. Simply repent of your past unholy life and begin to trust, rely upon, and strive to obey the Lord. That is, simply enlist into the kingdom of God. Then, immediately seek a good Bible-teaching, faith-walking local church.

By the way, congratulations if you have made the kingdom of God your choice! For when you accepted Jesus as savior and lord of your life, you made the greatest decision humanly possible. May the blessings of our Lord and God of all be with you and remain upon you forever. Amen!

CHAPTER SEVEN

Epilogue

This epilogue may appear to be a misfit at first glance, but it is quite relevant in that it provides food for thought to many otherwise skeptics. The Bible tells us, "The fool hath said in his heart, There is no God" (Ps. 14:1). Those are not necessarily bad people; some are merely skeptical. So I wish to offer a sampler of food for thought.

Although science attaches man's logic to many of the mysterious phenomena, most of us never embrace many of those things in our hearts. The best antidote for biblical skepticism is to spend lots of time viewing the *Discovery Channel* and the *Animal Channel* on television. Science reveals discoveries time after time that discredit evolution tremendously and support the ideas of the very creation it speaks against. It is important that we not demand all realities to mold themselves into our sphere of thinking and understanding. There are far too many mysterious phenomena in and around this world for us to try to either comprehend or understand and attach logic to.

Speaking of logical and illogical matters, a particular case comes to mind. No one was ever able to give a logical answer as to how a small dog some years ago rode from San Diego, California, to some place in Colorado in an automobile to its newly assigned home with a different family because its original owners were moving into a home where they were not allowed to have pets. Apparently, the little dog wished very, very much to be with its original owners. Anyway, weeks later, that little fellow showed up at the front door of the new home of its original owners. Its little feet were raw from traveling. But not only did the dog find its way back to San Diego, the little fellow did not stop until he located his former owners, who had moved to a new neighborhood. How logical is that? But it is a fact. The dog could not get directions by reading or asking questions, but he found that family.

According to the report relating to the dog, a family member opened the door there at their new dwelling place in San Diego (I do not recall if it was day or night), and there was the dog! And it was said that from then on the little dog was very troubled if it thought the lady of the house was about to leave it behind. The event is a fact—one that made many newspapers and other news media outlets. But such navigation by a little house dog truly does not seem logically possible. And there are thousands upon thousands of mysteries that make no sense. We are unable to assign logic to everything, but the facts of matters remain. More mysterious than the little dog, many other species exhibit numerous profound behaviors.

Many people are turned off from believing in life after death because they do not understand how the God we lift up and praise and trust so faithfully could be a true and eternal God and at the same time allow the misery to take place as it is being witnessed around the globe. And there is nothing wrong with taking those things into account. But know up front that doing so has not stopped anyone from dying, and it will not stop anyone from going to hell. What we need to do is try to get an understanding of the meaning of life and of death. We all bear witness that they both are taking place.

It is my desire that everyone gets an understanding that God loves them and that God is not a tyrant who wishes evil upon any person or thing. To the contrary, he has set principles and laws in motion that will deliver us from evil and into his wonderful eternal kingdom. All that we see in this earth has been established for the purpose of mankind. Everything created serves a purpose. Without many realizing it, that is why so much fuss is being made about preservation of various wildlife and plants. Many people understand the connection among all existence. Even the earthworm is here for man's benefit. You see, before the fall of man, it was not necessary for him to till the soil. Creatures like the earthworm were designed and assigned to prepare the soil for plant growth. For instance, the earthworm processes significant quantities of litter, which creates excellent topsoil. The worm also aerates soil, which also helps lessen its compaction. And today, many of us understand that interruption and destruction of plant and animal life on earth are upsetting the whole planet. This is because everything has been placed here with precision and purpose. But had the earth been forced to wait until the necessary objects evolved into being, life would have ceased to exist before it could have gotten started, in a manner of speaking.

What I wish to discuss primarily in this epilogue is the fact that the earth and all life therein are the result of intelligent design (my conviction is that it all happened on behalf of man). And the one behind this great design is the same one who designed the sum of the cosmos. The Bible says at Psalm 115:16, "The heaven, even the heavens (referring to the cosmos), are the Lord's: but the earth hath he given to the children of men." Thus, God wants man to rule and enjoy this earth, and he made it to be an everlasting habitation. Therefore, one must not think that natural death is final, nor should one be afraid that this earth or the sun or anything that God has made as an everlasting creation shall cease to exist, although the world of science says so. It sure enough may not sound logical that the earth could last forever, but neither does it sound logical that the earth came into existence in the first place. What is logical about the sun's having been in existence for more than four billion years—or however many it is said to have existed—or that it is predicted to last about that much longer and then burn out? This whole universe is the handiwork of God, and it is all mysterious. In light of the earth's being made for the habitation of mankind and everything in the earth being created in support of the welfare and comfort and enjoyment of man, God is not about to throw in the towel and call it quits.

Let us face reality: it is not logical that there could be one called Jehovah (God) who always exists, having neither beginning nor end. Nor is it logical that there could have been a spin-off or the beginning of existence at some distant point in the past, no matter how many trillions of years ago we assign to its beginning. The mystery would remain, "How could it have gotten started?" In the absence of anything, from where shall something come? And how about the one that used to play on my mind as I was growing up? I used to wonder what was behind the wall at the end of infinity. I still cannot comprehend infinity except as it pertains to a perfect circle. We can say it, but can we perceive there not being an end even if we could travel 180 degrees at the speed of light for trillions of years? But by being aware of your very own existence, you are a witness that life and tangible matter do exist, regardless from whence it came. Otherwise, you may as well deny your own existence. Chances are that we have all known people who pretended that their existence was only an illusion. In such cases, their sense of reason is the illusion.

What some skeptics seem to do is place the beginning in some distant past, far enough back that it alleviates having to deal with how existence got started in the first place. But as long as we consider something as being in the realm of time, we must also take into account the cause and effect. Something cannot come out of nothing unless it is created by something that has creative ability over "nothingness." Face it—if you are going to deal strictly by logic, simply put your finger on the basis from which all matter flows, assign the source and point from which its origin began, and explain how it is possible for something to proceed from absolutely nothing. That will compel you to look to God as the means, and it just might make a believer out of many skeptics.

When one stops and takes time to truly ponder the matter in his or her mind, it requires far more faith to believe in evolution than to believe in creationism. Creationism puts the cosmos into existence by intelligent design, whereas evolution, according the Darwinian theory, puts it into existence by mere chance. Christians rest on the belief that nothing is too hard for God and that all things that exist were made by him. We accept it by faith. But it is not that simple with the evolutionists. With them, line upon line and item upon item, everything that exists had to find its way into existence on its own accord, and it all happened by mere chance. But in order to be true to themselves and their belief, they need to account for how each type of species from all six biological kingdoms came into being.

Assume for a moment that the evolutionist is able to explain how each type of species from all the kingdoms came into existence. He still would not be able to explain how those things did so without certain vital parts and organs until they, on their own, figured out how to create necessities themselves or adapt themselves for survival (keep in mind that they are unintelligent creatures and plants). And the evolutionist must not stop there. He needs to explain how dumb plants and animals aligned themselves in such a chain of codependence with each other as studies reveal they do. For instance, if plants do not give off oxygen, animals cannot live. And if animals do not give off carbon dioxide, plants cannot survive. To top things off, the evolutionist needs to explain to us how all those species decided on their individual methods of procreation, seeing as there is no intelligent force behind them.

One of the interesting things about the evolutionists is that they claim to believe it all happened by mere chance, yet they are among the first to promote planet conservation. Everywhere I go, "green talk" is a focus. The US president recently visited Copenhagen, Denmark, addressing issues of global warming today. Gee, if everything exists as a result of things spinning and flying through the universe, why not let them keep moving? After all, if the universe has evolved this far on its own accord, things can only get better. Perhaps greenhouse gases will only cause the world to improve. I know that is a ridiculous pretense, but so is Darwin's theory of evolution.

Because the Christian-minded person can look into the heavenly space and also look down upon the earth and see the amazing handiworks of God and increase his faith in God, he is considered weak-minded by certain nonbelievers. But the question is, What kind of mind does it take to embrace the unsubstantiated, illogical claim of evolution? How smart is a mind like that? Something caused this world to exist as it does, and if there were no intelligent force behind it, there would have been no way for any matter, or even any "nothingness," to register in the first place. Using "logic," from whence could it have come? You can add as many trillion years to the equation as you wish, but at the very front of all those years, there still had to be a starting point. So reverse time (revert) to the beginning of those many, many trillions of years and explain the starting point. But consider that something cannot come out of nothing unless there is a stronger force or authority behind it all, and then pinpoint from whence that stronger force or authority came.

When one starts trying to explain away creation, there are some serious factors that must be taken into account. For starters, one must be ready to explain just how those millions upon millions of living creatures that require precise functions and exact timing of so many organs and body parts in order to exist from moment to moment managed to survive until everything came into place and became synchronized or fine tuned. It is too hard for me to comprehend just how all of those millions—actually, billions—of creatures were all struggling over the years to evolve into certain species, and all of a sudden the whole world became smart enough to know and respond to the fact that it had evolved far enough. Wow! That would mean we have a free-will world that has a mind and power of its own yet falls short of having the intellectual ability necessary to design. But as a reminder, the human body alone is so complex that it takes the study of many, many medical disciplines to learn and practice health care for people. And when you begin to consider all those other creatures, that turns out to be quite a thought! In fact, no one person can master the functions of the mind of the human being. The brain alone is too complex and too complicated and amazingly designed to have happened by mere chance.

One can discard the popular notion of there being life after death as much as one wishes, but that would be only an individual notion or belief. And I strongly urge you not to allow propaganda from the world of science to mislead you. The idea of creation does not complement science well enough to be promoted by it. Science must have logical explanations for all it embraces. It will assign an explanation and then make changes as knowledge progresses in those cases where it comes short of logical reasoning.

It was not long ago that many people professing to be eyewitnesses, including pilots, declared that they saw some sort of unidentified foreign object (UFO) that looked like a flying saucer over a certain large airport. They claimed they watched it ascend into the clouds and disappear, but the authorities said there was no such thing. The authorities went on to suggest that, chances are, the people saw a cloud just as it was doing a strange trick as the sun rays shined on it from a particular angle. Perhaps it was not any type of UFO, and I must admit that I have no clue as to what it might have been. But science must take the position that such is impossible unless someone can explain from where the object came. Truth does not matter with science. What does matter is that something can be explained, be it true or false.

I recall learning in my early years of public school that the earth was round, and by the time I finished high school, I was being told the earth was pear-shaped. In fact, well before I was born, the earth was thought to be a flat, four-cornered plane. And unless something happens whereby science can gather material proof of life after death, the great but skeptical minds will continue to dispute the idea of there being life after death. Yet if you would simply scrutinize and apply the knowledge you personally have of the arrangement of things in this earth—forget outer space—you too would have to acknowledge that there has to be an intelligent, almighty force involved in the creation and operation of our world. I have pondered over the matter and have concluded there is a true and living God of all. Therefore, my only approach to the life of the dead has to be from a godly perspective. That is, I am not wrestling with the opinion of whether or not there is a living God. I am convinced God is real.

It might not sound like it, considering what I am saying in this epilogue, but I believe very much in the discoveries of our scientists for the most part. It is because of what they have discovered and disclosed to us that makes me see such a glorious handiwork wrought by the mighty hand of God. I just finished previewing a book on apologetics that I am approving to become a textbook for the next semester of our Bible college. It contrasts or compares the size of the earth to that of the sun. In short, it states that 1,200,000 planets about the size of our earth could fit within the sun. From my personal study, I learned that the sun is about 109 times the size of the earth in diameter. And then there is a report that either the star Sirius A or Sirius B weighs 1,725 pounds per cubic inch. But that is not all; which ever one does not weigh 1,725 pounds weighs many times more than that. That is interesting, is it not? Let us reflect on this matter for a moment. It all connects to the question, "What is man?" God created all that mysterious stuff and still was not satisfied, in a sense, until he created man.

It is amazing, after considering the weight of all those stars and planets out there, that God keeps them in orbit or proper place. It has been explained to us that gravity keeps the earth in orbit. That is good. But after learning that it is so easy for a person to float away from the moon's surface, seeing that it also has a gravity pull, how is the force of gravity powerful enough to keep the moon in place yet not so strong that it could overpower an object such a human being who resists it? I imagine that it has to do with equal distribution of force. But there are lots of great objects in outer space that are stabilized and came from somewhere, and there is no place from whence to have come except a creator.

Planetary scientists have given numerous theories as to how the moon was created or formed. I will briefly mention four. (I am mentioning them only because I wish to make a point concerning the inaccuracy of a large portion of scientific reports as they fix space and matter to evolution.) The four I wish to mention are as follows: (1) the moon is the result of the coalescing of dust and gases as the solar system was being formed; (2) during the early formation of the earth, an unidentified planet crashed into earth and knocked almost a quarter of it loose, and that broken piece traveled almost 239,000 miles and somehow stopped and formed its own orbit; (3) when the earth was first flung (that means while it was still molten hot) from the sun, it was spinning so rapidly that a piece flung from it and formed the moon; and (4) the "fission theory," which suggests that the moon broke into two pieces, the greater piece forming the earth and the lesser piece forming the moon.

If we take into account any of the above four theories concerning the formation or creation of the moon, it does not contain factual integrity. For example, if the earth were flung from the sun, ended up forming an orbit path, and never stopped spinning, should not the moon have done the same thing, seeing that it traveled only a little less than 239,000 miles from the earth? They both would have gone through the same type and condition of space. They both would have contained the very same properties. By science's own reasoning, should not basically the same life forms exist on both due to what should have been the same atmospheric conditions? At least something should have developed. Yet, we have an earth with billions of life forms from both organisms and plants but a moon with none; and an earth with more than enough water, and a moon with practically none, if any. Lately, science has reported that perhaps the moon does not rotate as it was once thought to have done. (Maybe we have a change of fact.)

Many skeptics refute the words of the Holy Bible while they embrace whatever science reports. I wonder if any of them have stopped to consider that our Holy Bible has not published so much as "one change" in all of its existence? Yes, there have been mistranslations and misinterpretations found printed in perhaps every version. But the Holy Bible, the original script, the raw Word of God remains the same, while science is constantly updating its reports and making new suggestions almost daily, if not daily.

I used to perform a solo in my high school glee club choir for a song entitled "How Great Thou Art." The lyrics take notice of the heavenly creations and accredit them to the handiworks of God.

I often think of the song "How Great Thou Art" when I am considering the awesomeness of creation. According to science, the Milky Way Galaxy that we all study in grade school contains billions upon billions of stars. That is awesome! Science has determined that that galaxy alone measures in the neighborhood of ten thousand light years across. The length of it has been estimated to be ten times the width. That might not sound too amazing until you put it in a certain perspective. For instance, it takes only 1.25 seconds for light to travel between the earth and the moon. Now think of all the seconds contained in a calendar year (31,536,000) and then multiply each second by 186,000. That's a hint. There are slightly fewer than thirty-two million seconds in a calendar year. So, multiply that figure by 186,000, and you will come up with one light year. (I came up with 5,878,000,000,000 miles.) Then, multiply the miles you come up with for that one light year by the ten thousand light years it takes for light to move across the Milky Way. Next, multiply the width of the Milky Way Galaxy by ten to get the length of it. (I shall leave that one up to you.) But I will remind you that we have just hinted at the size of one of the billions of galaxies.

Let us now go beyond normal comprehension. To reach the next cluster of stars, you would have to travel 186,000 miles per second for the next million years. And we have not gotten warmed up yet. Remember, we are talking about billions and billions of galaxies. Our earth can fit inside many of those objects many times over. We get this report from science; we have no way of knowing how accurate the reports are. But assuming any degree of accuracy, it should create awe in the mind of anyone who can remotely comprehend what that means. Could you still think all that happened by mere chance?

The reports of the size and approximate distance of the galaxies are, as far as I know, accepted by most people, and I have no basis upon which to refute them. Of course, some of them are likely to be far-fetched, but for the most part, they are believable. But how can anyone believe a small part of this story and believe at the same time in evolution? The more phenomenal the reports that science gives are, the more they reinforce my conviction concerning creation.

Can you believe that matter created itself out of nothing? After all, every report suggests that matter came before life. Do not tell me that matter came from some source of gas. Gas is also matter. Even if you say it all came from nothing, I would like to know what gave nothing the notion to become something. I am not trying to sound facetious. I just need to make a point. Evolution suggests that everything has a beginning and an end, be it ever so many trillions of years between the beginning and now or start and finish.

Of course, modern science suggests that matter came from compacted atoms. But keep in mind that science once taught that matter could neither be created nor destroyed. Later, we began to hear that matter can be destroyed. But I believe that matter cannot be destroyed nor created except by God. We probably can blast it into a form we have not yet been able to detect. Think about, for a period of time, how on one hand you are told that matter cannot be created or destroyed and, in the same breath, you are told that everything came into existence apart from intelligent creation. Perhaps someone meant that only matter could create itself. (I am only pointing these things out to remind us just how gullible we can allow ourselves to become.)

Living organisms undergo various transformations and changes for the purpose of adaptation and accommodation, but evolutionists are quick to call such activity a matter of evolving from one species to another. I am not aware of any bona fide proof of animals' evolving from one species to another so as to become a human being. Yet people are set on the idea that man evolved from some lower animal. It should not be a strange notion that physical changes are subject to take place in certain living organisms. I say again, the reason for the change would stem from a change in environment, in climate, or in behavior and the like. Even if the dolphin becomes as smart as man and develops feet, legs, and arms, it will still not be a man. Man is a spirit that comes from the breath of God. Believe it or not, you came from the breath of God. You are eternal. It is up to you to choose where and how you shall spend eternity.

CPSIA information can be obtained at www.ICGtesting.com
230074LV00002B/9/P